The Clash of Civilisations

An Islamic View

by

Dr. Abū Ameenah Bilal Philips

ISBN 978 1 898649 71 7

British Library Cataloguing in Publication Data.
A catalogue record for this book is available from the British Library.

Published by: Al-Hidaayah Publishing and Distribution Ltd

Distributed by: Al-Hidaayah Publishing and Distribution Ltd
P.O. Box 3332
Birmingham
United Kingdom
B10 0UH

Tel: 0121 753 1889
Fax: 0121 753 2422
Website: www.al-hidaayah.co.uk
Email: mail@al-hidaayah.co.uk

The Clash of Civilisations
An Islamic View

Contents

Transliteration Table

Consonants,

ء	’	د	d	ض	ḍ	ك	k
ب	b	ذ	dh	ط	ṭ	ل	l
ت	t	ر	r	ظ	ẓ	م	m
ث	th	ز	z	ع	‘	ن	n
ج	j	س	s	غ	gh	ه	h
ح	ḥ	ش	sh	ف	f	و	w
خ	kh	ص	ṣ	ق	q	ي	y

Vowels, diphthongs, etc.

Short:	ـَ	a	ـِ	i	ـُ	u
Long:	ـَا	ā	ـِي	ī	ـُو	ū
diphthongs:			ـَى	ay	ـَو	aw

Introduction

It is important to understand Islām from a cultural point of view because the basis of much of the current turmoil within Muslim countries and conflict with their neighbours can be attributed to cultural clashes. Consequently, a clear understanding of culture and its derivatives is necessary to comprehend the relevance of Islām to the civilisation of Muslim peoples in the twentieth century and beyond.

The word "culture" comes from the Latin *cultura* which is a derivative of the verb *colere* meaning "tending" or "cultivation." It was first recorded in the Oxford Dictionary of English in 1510 as meaning: "training of the mind" or "manners."[1] However, culture in anthropological usage, may be defined as "the way of life of a specific group."[2]

> "Basically, the idea of culture arises from the observation that what human beings do and what they refrain from doing is, in part, a consequence of being brought up in one group as opposed to another. People have a social heredity as well as a biological heredity."[3]

Biological heredity represents practices common to all human societies, like, sleep, marriage, care for children and smiling,

---

[1] *Colliers Encyclopedia*, vol. 7, Macmillan Educational Company, NY, 1989, p. 560.

[2] Ibid., p. 558. While virtually all students of man agree upon the indispensable importance of the concept of culture, no single definition has yet won universal acceptance.

[3] Ibid., p. 558.

while social heredity refers to customs which usually vary from one society to the next. A simple definition of culture would then be 'the man-made part of the human environment.' "Members of the human species are trained in the family and in their education, formal and informal, to behave in ways that are conventional and fixed by tradition."[4]

The culture of most of the world today is that of Western Europe and America. It was exported to the remainder of the world during the period of European colonization and continued during the neo-colonial era by way of indirect rule. In the twentieth century, Western culture has been promoted on a massive scale through the far-reaching effects of the media. Today, it is not surprising to find in the pages of National Geographic pictures of South American Indian youths in loin cloth in the middle of the Amazon wearing baseball caps with a *Nike* logo or Mongolian horsemen in the middle of the Gobi Desert wearing striped *Adidas* sweat pants and *Reebok* trainers. Western culture now represents the dominant cultural influence in most countries, both non-Muslim and Muslim. And it is the natural conflict that arises from the clash of cultures, which dominate the social and political policies in both the West and the East. Harvard University Professor, Samuel P. Huntington summed up the essential issues of the cultural clash in his following observation:

> "The underlying problem for the West is not Islamic fundamentalism. It is Islam, a different civilisation whose people are convinced of the superiority of their culture and are obsessed with the inferiority of their power. The problem for Islam is not CIA or the U.S. Department of defence. It is the West, a different civilisation whose people are convinced of the universality of their culture and believe that their superior, if declining, power imposes on them the obligation

[4] *Colliers Encyclopedia*, vol. 7, p. 558.

> to impose that culture throughout the world. These are the basic ingredients that fuel conflict between Islam and the West."[5]

In this statement, Professor Huntington dismisses the usual claims regarding Islamic fundamentalist terrorism as the major threat to the New World Order. Western media constantly reduces the world's problems to this common denominator. *The New York Times* carried an article stating that:

> "Muslim fundamentalism is fast becoming the chief threat to global peace and security as well as the cause of national and local disturbance through terrorism. It is akin to the menace posed by Nazism and fascism in the 1930's and then by communism in the 50's."[6]

However, Professor Huntington brushes such claims aside and identifies Islām itself as the main problem for the West because its civilisation is fundamentally different from Western civilisation. He also identified two distinct qualities of Muslims which, in his opinion, contribute to the problem. The first is that Muslims consider their culture superior to all other cultures. Most Muslims will openly claim that Islām is better than all other religions and philosophies. This attitude is a natural consequence of their belief that the religion of Islām was revealed from God. It is only logical to assume that the culture created by practising God's religion must, of necessity, be superior to any culture resulting from human experiment.

The other quality is that Muslims desire that the laws that govern them be Islamic. Much of the turmoil in the Muslim world today, in Algeria, Egypt, Chechnya, Dagestan, etc., is a direct result of this desire. During the era of European colonization

---

[5] *The Clash of Civilisations*, pp. 217-8.

[6] *The New York Times / International Herald Tribune,* 9/9/93

of the Muslim world, the colonial administration substituted European laws for Islamic law. During the neo-colonial era, Muslims who were trained by their colonial masters were given the reins of government of Muslim territories and continued to govern according to European law. Today, the vast majority of Muslim governments rule according to British, French, German and Dutch laws, and Muslim law is only partially applied in the area of family law. Consequently, as the wave of Islamic awareness sweeps over the Muslim world, the aspiration of Muslims for self-determination has exploded in a series of violent confrontations with existing administrations. In places like Indonesia, where since the era of Sukarno (1945 – 1965) and his successor Suharto (1968 - 1998), Pancasilia,[7] has been the state philosophy/religion taught in all schools to the population of some 200 million Indonesians, 95% of whom are Muslims. And, to suggest that Islamic law be introduced was considered an act of treason. In 1998, Suharto was finally overthrown by popular dissent. All of those who clamoured for power, including Suharto's henchman and substitute, B.J. Habibe, immediately began paying some allegiance to Islām. And in recent elections, Sukarno's daughter, Megawati Sukarnoputri, was decisively defeated by Nahdlatul ʿUlama's ʿAbdur Raḥmān Wāhid, who is half-blind and can hardly walk.

On the other hand, Professor Huntington negates the Central Intelligence Agency (CIA) as the chief enemy of Muslims. Although the CIA has a reputation for toppling governments and assassinating political figures, the professor assures Muslims that it is not their chief enemy. He further rules out the American

---

[7] Literally, "The Five Principles". Sukarno first articulated it in June 1, 1945 to the preparatory committee for independence, sponsored by the Japanese during World War II. He argued that the future Indonesian state should be based on the Five Principles: Indonesian nationalism; humanism; democracy; social prosperity; and belief in one God (*The New Encyclopaedia Britannica*, vol. 9, p. 108).

military complex in spite of its presence in Saudi Arabia, its decimation of the Iraqi army, its launching of cruise missiles into the Sudan and Afghanistan, and its open support for Israel. The real source of the problem facing the Muslim World, according to Professor Huntington, is Western civilisation itself. He further explains that the root of the problem lies in the fact that the West considers its culture superior to all other cultures. It considers its civilisation and its leading principles something that all human beings should aspire for and live by. Why? Because, according to Darwinian theory, the evolutionary process refines and improves human beings and their society. From our supposed savage ape-like origins to twentieth century civility, human society has progressed relentlessly. During the last few centuries, the evolutionary principle of "survival of the fittest" appear to have placed Western nations and their culture at the top of the pyramid of human civilisation. Thus, claims the West, the foundational principles of their civilisation must be the most suitable for human society. Professor Huntington takes the issue another step further, pointing out that the West not only considers its culture the most appropriate for all nations, but it considers itself duty bound to impose their culture by any means necessary, politically or militarily, on the rest of the world. These have been correctly identified by Professor Huntington as the essential elements of the cultural clash facing the world as it enters the 21st century.

Consequently, the central theme of this book, which focuses on the foundations of Islamic culture, will first be preceded by a brief look at the foundations of Western culture.

The Foundations of Western Culture

The roots of Western culture can be found in Europe. Western civilisation is often referred to as being a Greco-Roman civilisation. It began in Greece and Rome while the rest of Europe existed in a state of savagery. However, as in the rest of Europe, their official religion was one of idolatry. The Greeks and Romans worshipped a multitude of gods, all distinguished from men by their immortality. They were thought to control various natural or social forces: Zeus the weather, Poseidon the sea, Demeter the harvest, Hera marriage, Fortuna good and bad fortune, Diana love, and so on. In Greek mythology, the major gods lived on Mount Olympus led by the chief god, Zeus (Jupiter in Rome). All gods were worshipped as idols in human form and the most important act of Greek worship was the sacrifice. Sacrificial offerings varied according to the gods addressed: e.g. cows for Hera, bulls for Zeus, and pigs for Demeter.[8]

Effects

The effects of idolatry from Greece and Rome, as well as other European nations, can still be found in Western civilisation, though the religions have long since been abandoned. For example, although each country around the world today has names for the days of the week in their own language, the English names for the days of the week have become the international standard.

---

[8] *The New Encyclopaedia Britannica,* vol. 5, p. 462.

The origin of the English names is bathed in idolatry. The days assigned by the Romans for the worship of the Sun, Moon, and Saturn were retained for the corresponding days of the week; Saturday from the Old English term *Saeterndaeg,* or Saturn's day (Saturn being the Roman god of agriculture), Sunday from Old English *sunnan daeg,* day of the sun; Monday from Old English *monandaeg,* moon day. The other weekday names are derived from Anglo-Saxon words for the gods of Teutonic mythology. Tuesday is derived from Old English *Tiwesdaeg,* Tiw's day (Tiw being the Anglo-Saxon name for Tyr, the Norse god of war); Wednesday from Old English *Wodnes daeg,* the day of Woden (the chief god of the Germanic peoples); Thursday from Old English *thunresdaeg,* the day of Thunor [Thor], the Anglo-Saxon god of thunder; and Friday from Old English *Frigedaeg,* the goddess Frig's day (Frigg was the wife of Woden, and she was the goddess of beauty and love).[9]

Western civilisation also identifies its roots as being Judeo-Christian. Christianity's origins are in Judaism. Jesus was a Jewish prophet who lived according to Jewish Law (The Torah). However, Jesus' teachings were paganised when they were transferred to Greece and Rome. The Roman and Greek gods looked like human beings and were known to have relations with humans producing half-gods. In the new teachings, Jesus became God incarnate, born of a human mother who walked the earth among humans. Statues of Jesus, his mother, and the saints became an integral part of Christian worship. The main day for congregational worship was shifted from the Sabbath (Saturday) to Sunday. In Rome, Sunday was the day designated for the worship of the Sun god, Apollo, the son of the chief god, Jupiter. The shift was to attract Roman pagans based on the similarity in their beliefs about the son of god.

---

[9] *Chambers Pocket Dictionary,* W & R Chambers Ltd., Edinburgh, 1992, and *The New Encyclopaedia Britannica,* vol. 12, p. 555.

Christmas (from Old English *Cristes maesse,* "Christ's mass") is another example of the paganisation of Christianity. The 25th of December was chosen by the Roman Catholic Church as the date of Jesus' birth without any scriptural or historical evidence. The earliest record of its celebration was in AD 336 in Rome.[10] The 25th coincided with the pagan Roman festival marking the "birthday of the unconquered sun" (*natalis solis invicti*); this festival celebrated the winter solstice, when the days again begin to lengthen. It also coincided with Roman celebration of the Saturnalia (17th December) in which gifts were exchanged.[11] Tree worship, common among the pagan Europeans, survived after their conversion to Christianity in the Scandinavian customs of decorating the house and barn with ever greens (Christmas trees).[12]

Furthermore, a traveller in the West will not find in the elevators of apartment buildings, commercial complexes or hotels, a 13th floor. Houses on streets are numbered: 11,12, 12 ½, 14. No one wants to live in house number 13, apartment number 13 or floor number 13. During the late 60's, an Apollo moonshot missed the moon and was almost lost in space but narrowly managed to return to earth safely. After its crew were fished out of the Atlantic and brought back to the Cape Canaveral base, reporters questioned the flight commander about his feelings. He replied that he should have known that this would have happened. When they quizzed him about details of technical problems that were ignored, he replied that there were none. Instead, he informed them that the flight was Apollo 13, which took off at 13:13 hours on Friday the 13th! This superstition has its roots in Christian tradition that holds that at the Last Supper Jesus ate with his

---

[10] The Eastern Roman Empire celebrated it on the 6th of January.

[11] *The New Encyclopaedia Britannica,* vol. 3, p. 283.

[12] Ibid., p. 284.

twelve disciples. One of them, Judas, later betrayed Jesus leading to his apparent crucifixion. Thirteen, as it turned out, was bad luck for Jesus; consequently, pagan beliefs in good and bad luck charms resurfaced among Westerners in number 13.

The Holy Roman Empire

> "The heritage of Rome was fused with the Germanic and Christian elements to provide the medieval foundations of Western civilisation."[13]

Distorted Christianity in the form of the Roman Catholic Church ruled Europe along with temporal kings and emperors during the Middle Ages.[14] The Renaissance or "Re-birth" represented a casting off of the shackles of Roman Catholic dogma that had long stifled and crushed independent thought and any attempt at scientific inquiry and reform. Church scholars as well as scientists who questioned any aspect of the teachings accepted by the Roman Catholic Church-State were branded heretics and were often tortured or burned at the stake. And that period of church rule subsequently become known as "the Dark Ages." Two distinct trends in the context of religion were produced by the Renaissance movement; one of reform lead by Martin Luther (1483-1546) and Calvin (1509-1564) and the other of total rejection lead by the likes of Hume (1711-1776). The reform movement which became known as the Protestant movement, rejected the accumulated rites, rituals and hierarchy of Roman Catholicism in an attempt to

---

[13] *The New Encyclopaedia Britannica,* vol. 18, p. 605.

[14] The period in European history from the fall of the Western Roman Empire (*c.* AD 395) to the period of the Renaissance (*c.* 14th century). It was coined by Italian humanists to distinguish themselves from the thousand-year period of darkness and ignorance (the Dark Ages) separating them from the ancient Greek and Roman world whose learning and culture they sought to revive. (*The New Encyclopaedia Britannica,* vol. 8, p. 107).

return to a purer form of Christianity. After a bitter struggle with church leaders leading to the excommunication of many reformers, a number of communities throughout Europe broke off and formed new churches in which Mary the mother of Jesus was no longer worshipped and intercession through saints was no longer sought. Priests were allowed to marry and the infallibility of the authority of the Pope was totally rejected. Rites like communion in which little pieces of bread were served to the congregation in the belief that the pieces were somehow transformed into the body of Jesus Christ, were dropped along with the use of Latin in church rites. On the other hand, the total rejection movement denied or questioned the existence of God and with it the validity of religion. It became popular among philosophical circles of that period to deny God's existence. And, for the first time in recorded history, pure atheism began to be propagated on a wide scale. At first it was done quietly, but eventually it spread and became openly stated, especially in scientific and political circles.

The great transition to modern science occurred in the battle over Copernicus's theory – the Copernican revolution. Galileo was the hero of this great battle. He claimed that the observations of the heavens he had made with his new telescope vindicated Copernicus's theory: Contrary to what people had thought for centuries, the sun was fixed and the earth orbited around it and rotated on an axis. This novel idea was annoying to the followers of Aristotle who conspired against him to get the Church to silence him and ultimately convict him as a heretic.[15] In so doing, the Church forever discredited its doctrines in the minds of many thinking people. It sacrificed its claim that it had a monopoly on the truth.

Galileo was punished and his books officially banned. But his ideas triumphed, and with them came the end of Aristotelian

---

[15] *The Truth in the Light,* pp. 45-46.

science and the search for final causes. In time, scientists were able to elaborate more and more mechanisms to explain how the universe and everything we see around us worked. All the mysteries that human beings had once attributed to God or the gods turned out to have simple mechanistic explanations.

As the mechanistic explanation expanded, it left increasingly little room for God. By the 18th century, theism (belief in a personal God) had given way to deism – or the view of God as simply the "first cause" and underlying principle of rationality in the universe.[16] The most famous 18th century deist, Voltaire, openly attacked religion. Deism quickly deteriorated into atheism, or the belief in no God at all. Such was the position of the English philosopher David Hume.[17]

Until the 19th century, the vast majority of people and even a significant portion of the intellectual elite remained religious believers. Then came the final blow: the coming of age of the two "historical" sciences, geology and biology. In the early 19th century, many scientists still thought the Old Testament gave the literal account of the early history of the world, and they came up with a history of the earth based on the first books of the Bible. They computed the age of the earth from the biblical genealogies. They explained the irregularities of the earth with reference to Noah's flood. The theory was known as *catastrophism* and its proponents saw it as a way of vindicating belief in God with reference to nature. In 1830, Charles Lyell's book *Principles of Geology* blew the catastrophists out of the water. In three volumes of meticulous argumentation, Lyell showed how the normal forces of nature could account for all the irregularities of the natural landscape – so long as one assumed that the earth was vastly older than the Bible stories suggested.[18]

---

[16] *The Truth in the Light,* p. 214.

[17] *God The Evidence,* p. 34.

[18] *The Truth in The Light,* p. 213.

Lyell's geology did to the Protestant world what Galileo's discoveries had done to the Catholic one.[19] By the middle of the 19th century, educated people were finding it extremely difficult to reconcile the discoveries of the new science with religious faith. The trauma could be seen in the work of Victorian England's most popular poet, Alfred Tennyson, who described a new vision of nature as "red in tooth and claw." in *In Memoriam* dedicated to the untimely death of his closest friend.

The young Darwin took the first volume of Lyell's *Principles of Geology* along on his famous voyage on the *Beagle* in 1831. He went into the voyage a Bible-believing Christian; within a short time after the voyage, he was agnostic.[20] He would not publish *The Origin of Species* until 1859. When it appeared, it was the *coup de grace*: Modern science had at last found a simple mechanism to explain the origin of life and the human species itself. Darwin breathed fresh life into the atheist position – a fact immediately recognised across the globe. Notably, the famous 19th century atheist, Karl Marx, asked Darwin if he could dedicate the English translation of *Capital* to him. In the German edition, he wrote "From a devoted admirer of Charles Darwin."

Science, it appeared, had found mechanistic explanations for everything. The verdict seemed inescapable. It was uttered finally in 1885 by the German philosopher Freidrich Nietzsche, the philosophical "shock jock" of his era: "God is dead."[21]

Both Darwin's Theory of Evolution and Marx's Theory of Dialectical Materialism attempted to explain human existence in terms of natural and socio-economic forces thereby removing the need for relying on supernatural forces for its explanations. In his book, *The Origin of the Species*, Darwin implied that humans

---

[19] *God The Evidence,* p. 35.

[20] *Broca's Brain,* pp. 301-311.

[21] *God The Evidence,* p. 37.

shared their origin with the ape which, like all other forms of multi-cellular life, evolved from unicellular organisms through a process which he named "natural selection" but which became commonly known as "Survival of the fittest." Marx in turn reduced all of human history to an economic struggle between the haves and the have-nots; empty stomachs and full stomachs or as he called it "class struggle". All social systems to Marx were expressions of one or another of the two classes, the ruling class and the oppressed class. Thus, religion in Marx's analysis was a tool used by the ruling class to maintain the status quo and God was the fictitious friend of the rich who pre-destined their rule over the poor.

Darwinism

Darwin regarded white Europeans as more "advanced" than other human races. While Darwin presumed that man evolved from ape-like creatures, he surmised that some races developed more than others and that the latter still bore simian features. In his book, *The Decent of Man*, which he published after *The Origin of Species*, he boldly commented on "the greater differences between men of distinct races".[22]

In pre-Victorian England, Darwin's thoughts about dark-skinned natives prevailed, providing new footing for racism and in turn imperialism and colonization. Darwin's views gave a pseudo-biological rationale, a scientific veneer, to Europeans marching into the underdeveloped lands of Africa, Asia and the Pacific to plunder their peoples and their resources... Progressive imperialists explained that their mission was to civilize the natives, those backward unfortunates on the lower rungs of man's evolutionary ladder.[23]

---

[22] *What Darwin Really Said,* pp. 54-56.

[23] *The Genesis Mystery,* by Jeffery Goodman (Times Books, 1983) quoted in *Clinging To A Myth,* p. 9.

Secular Democracy

The main banner of Western Civilisation today is that of secular democracy. It is held up by Western nations as the ideal for all societies of the world to follow. Since the most advanced societies, according to the Western view, are those of the West, the systems which they have developed must also be the most advanced and appropriate for modern human society.

Secularism is a system of beliefs which rejects all forms of religious faith and worship. It is also the view that public education and other matters of civil policy should be conducted without the introduction of a religious element.[24] In the medieval period, there was a strong tendency for religious persons to despise human affairs and to meditate on God and the afterlife. As a reaction to this medieval tendency, secularism, at the time of the Renaissance, exhibited itself in the development of humanism,[25] when man began to show more interest in human cultural achievements and the possibilities of his fulfilment in this world. The movement toward secularism has been in progress during the entire course of modern history.[26]

One of the novel features of European civilisation in the later 16th and 17th centuries was a secularization of mental interests. Secular learning could now produce ideas more fascinating to intelligent men than theology.[27]

Toward the end of the Middle Ages, there was a renewed interest in those studies that stressed the importance of man,

---

[24] *The Living Webster Encyclopedic Dictionary of the English Language*, p. 869.

[25] The word *humanism* comes from *studia humanitatis* (studies of humanity).

[26] *The New Encyclopaedia Britannica,* vol. 10, p. 594.

[27] Ibid., vol. 20, p. 569.

his faculties, affairs, worldly aspirations, and well-being. The primacy of theology and other worldliness was over; the "reducing everything to a theological argument" was rejected since it no longer expressed the reality of the new situation that was developing in Europe. Society had been profoundly transformed, commerce had expanded, and life in the cities had evolved. Economic and political power, previously in the hands of the ecclesiastical hierarchy and the feudal lords, was beginning to be taken over by the city burghers.[28]

The Greek conception of natural law was refined by the Stoic school of philosophy (4th century BC). The Stoics posited that the existence of an innate reason in men linked everyone with the cosmic order and subjected all to a universally valid moral law. This concept thoroughly infused Roman thinking.

In the Middle Ages, St. Augustine of Hippo, placed God's reason beside God's will as the highest source of the unchangeable, eternal, divine law binding directly on man and all other creatures. The divine law was thus accessible to both man's reason and his faith and was not, as St. Paul had largely concluded, the product of his will alone and hence not rational in terms of human as opposed to divine reason. At a second level, Augustine placed the no less unchangeable natural law, being the divine law as man is given reason, heart, and soul to understand it. The third level of temporal, or positive, law was warranted by the eternal divine law, even though it changed from time to time and from place to place, so long as it respected the limits laid down by the divine and natural law.

The concept of secularism is in direct conflict with the foundations of Islamic Civilisation. Faith and worship are interwoven into the fabric of Islamic society. Islamic law in the

---

[28] *The New Encyclopaedia Britannica,* vol. 18, p. 27.

Muslim nation governs both education and civil policy. To rule by other than divinely revealed law is considered an act of corruption and disbelief. This principle is clearly stated in the Qur'ān:

وَمَن لَّمْ يَحْكُم بِمَآ أَنزَلَ ٱللَّهُ فَأُو۟لَٰٓئِكَ هُمُ ٱلْكَٰفِرُونَ

"Whoever does not judge by what Allāh revealed is a disbeliever." Sūrah *al-Mā'idah* (5):44.

The difference in view is a product of a difference in understanding of the purpose of human existence. Islām holds that human beings were created by God to live righteous lives during their limited stay on earth in order to enjoy a blissful eternal life in the hereafter. The divinely prescribed acts of worship guide humans to righteousness. Therefore, divinely revealed religion has a role to play in all facets of human life:

قُلْ إِنَّ صَلَاتِى وَنُسُكِى وَمَحْيَاىَ وَمَمَاتِى لِلَّهِ
رَبِّ ٱلْعَٰلَمِينَ ﴿١٦٢﴾

"Say: Indeed my prayers, sacrifices, living and dying are for Allāh, Lord of all worlds." Sūrah *al-An'ām* (6):162.

In secular democracies, humans are a product of the evolutionary process having no more purpose than the other animals around them: "Eat, drink and be merry for tomorrow you may die." According to this view, religion only hinders human freedom to enjoy this life. Therefore, it should be completely side lined. Those who wish to limit themselves may do so, while others should be free to live their lives without religious interference. Instead, humans would limit themselves by their own choosing in accordance to principles of their own choosing. The method of choosing would be democracy or majority rule.

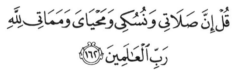

Democracy

Both the name and concept of democracy originated in ancient Greece. It meant "rule of the people." In the Greek city-states, particularly Athens, slaves and women were excluded from the vote so only a minority of the inhabitants (20-30%) were active citizens.[29] The realities of Western democracies today are not much different. In fact, the minority which rules has become even smaller. The United States of America goes through the motions of elections, in order to give the population the illusion that it participates actively in governing itself. The absence of free education from kindergarten to Ph.D. ensures that the mass of society cannot participate in government. The high cost of tertiary education also prevents most people from the lower classes from elevating themselves in society. However, if a poll were taken among American citizens, the vast majority would favour free education, free health care and subsidized housing. Free education stops at the end of high school not because it is economically impossible to continue, but because it is necessary to keep the majority dependent on the explanations of the minority. Countries like Sudan have managed to provide free education in spite of their economic difficulties.

Democracy, as perceived by Western thinkers, is not merely a political tool, but a social principle and philosophy. They boldly state that "Western democracy reaches beyond the confines of government and affects all phases of human relations."[30]

Democracy as a way of life is based on three main principles. The first principle is that of Equality. From the rationalist humanist viewpoint, all humans have, over and above differences

---

[29] *Colliers Encyclopedia*, vol. 8, p. 76 and 80.

[30] It holds that reason is applicable not only to the understanding and mastery of nature, but also to the understanding and conduct of social problems.

of class, race, sex, nationality and religion, one common trait; the ability to reason.[31] This principle is not in opposition to Islamic teachings. However, the emphasis on equality in Islām lies in the belief in God. The Prophet was quoted as saying, "*Every child is born with a natural belief in God* (*fiṭrah*)."[32]

The second principle of rational empiricism fundamentally implies full confidence in human reason and experience. It is supposed that the human mind has the ability to deduce from historical and personal experience what is in fact best for human society. However, this is not really the case. For example, the American Constitution, written by the best and most trusted minds of the eighteenth century, contains an article which is so fundamentally unjust and incorrect, that it defies comprehension by the modern enlightened mind. Article 1, section 2, entitled The Three-Fifth Compromise stated that black men (slaves at the time) were to be counted as three-fifth of a white man.[33] Its authors all were slave owners who did not consider their slaves their equal. Consequently, when writing that document they merely expressed the ideas and beliefs of the ruling class of their times. Human reason and experience failed to arrive at what was in fact just. Any review of the legal systems of Europe, Asia or Africa all indicate that human lawmakers make laws according to their own sectarian or class interests. They have great difficulty in being truly objective. Consequently, Islamic civilisation holds

---

[31] *Colliers Encyclopedia*, vol. 8, p. 77.

[32] *Ṣaḥīḥ Al Bukhāri*, no. 1296.

[33] Constitution of the United States of America 1787, Article 1, section 2 states: "[Representatives and direct Taxes shall be apportioned among the several States which may be included within this Union, according to their respective Numbers, which shall be determined by adding to the whole number of free Persons, including those bound to Service for a Term of Years, and excluding Indians not taxed, three fifths of all other Persons.]" Source: U.S. Government Printing Office 1988 – 203 – 017 / 80002.

that only God, who created human beings, knows their needs and who has no vested interests in any class, can legislate absolutely fair laws. Human input is restricted to the implementation of the divine laws and the deduction of secondary laws.

The third principle is referred to as Discussion and Consent. It is the mechanism by which democratic decisions are made. Discussion is based on the democratic view that no one possesses absolute truth, therefore, all sides to an argument must be given free expression. No truth is so certain that it may not be challenged."[34] After hearing everyone's view, decisions are made by majority vote. Consequently, truth, falsehood, good and evil all become relative. As is often said, "One man's meat is another man's poison". Furthermore, what is good today can become evil tomorrow and vice versa. The social consequence of this principle is the removal of any foundation for stable morals in society. For example, the book *Catcher in the Rye* which was declared pornographic and banned in the fifties is currently required reading in Canadian high schools. Since 1976, every issue of a mainstream British newspaper, *The Sun*, contains nude and semi-nude photographs of females on page 3. Similar pictures in *Playboy* magazines caused it to be labelled pornographic in the sixties.

Another classic case in point, is that of the homosexual onslaught in the latter part of the 20th century. If the average Westerner were asked about his or her view on homosexuality in the 50's and 60's, they would immediately respond that it was sick, degenerate, perverse, etc.. If they were religious they might even quote the Bible in which it is referred to as "an abomination unto the Lord." Psychiatrists of that period included it in their main reference works as a mental illness with suggested treatments ranging from shock therapy to drug therapy. However, if the same question was asked in the 70's and early 80's, the response would

---

[34] *Colliers Encyclopedia*, vol. 8, p. 77.

have been that homosexuality is a personal choice, an alternative lifestyle, "different strokes for different folks", etc.. Consequently, homosexuality has been stricken from the Psychiatrist's Bible, only to be replaced by another illness called *homophobia*. Those who despise homosexuality and those who practise it are now labelled "homophobic" and are sent to the psychiatrist's couch for treatment. Western civilisation swung from one extreme end of the moral spectrum to the opposite end based on its democratic principles.

During the fifties and sixties, a sexual revolution began in the West culminating in the removal of fornication and adultery from the law books as punishable crimes. When modern Western legislators analysed fornication and marriage, they concluded that the only difference between the two was a piece of paper; the marriage certificate. It was only religious influence (The Ten Commandments) that had made fornication illegal. During that period, lawmakers deduced a new principle to determine the legality of sexual relations between people. Since rape was unanimously considered unacceptable, they concluded that the principle of "consent" must be present for such relations to be legally acceptable. They also all agreed that sexual relations between adults and children were wrong (paedophilia) since children could easily be taken advantage of by adults due to their immaturity. Consequently, they added the second principle of "adulthood" for legal sexual relations. The phrase "consenting adults"[35] became the battle cry of the sexual revolution resulting in

[35] "In recent years, in Europe and the United States, a number of highly respected legal, medical, and religious organizations have deliberated on the whole issue of the legal control of human sexuality. They have been unanimous in the conclusion that, while the laws protecting person and public sensibilities should be retained, *the purely moral laws should be dropped. Specifying what consenting adults do sexually in private, it is argued, should not be subject to legal control.*" (*The New Encyclopaedia Britannica*, vol. 27, p. 247).

an upsurge or wife swapping parties, group sex, sadomasochism, topless bars, etc., among many elements of the society.

Paralleling the sexual revolution during the sixties was the Civil Rights Movement. Black Americans had become fed up with social and economic discrimination and took to the streets in protest. Many neighbourhoods were burnt down in major American cities across the United States in their quest for civil rights. Finally, the American establishment made the necessary amendments to laws to provide a legal basis for opposing racial discrimination. Towards the end of the Civil Rights Era, women began to demand their rights. They had played a major role in the Civil Rights struggle; in fact the catalyst for the struggle was Rosa Parks' refusal to sit at the back of a bus in Montgomery, Alabama, December 1955 which ignited the flame of protest.[36] Women began to demand the right of equal pay for equal work as well as the right to hold any position men traditionally held. The women's movement met with great success and amendments were made in state legislature to ensure women's rights. Following their success, homosexuals began to assert themselves, demanding an end to nation-wide discrimination against them. There were state laws which barred them from holding a number of posts. During this period many began to come out of the proverbial closet and into the streets in protest. At first, the lawmakers balked. Homosexuality was a no-no. American society from its inception abhorred such practices. However, the homosexuals raised the sexual revolution's banner of "consenting adults" and openly challenged the mores of society. They reminded the lawmakers that objection to homosexuality was religious based, and religion was not supposed to interfere in people's private or public lives in a secular democracy. Eventually, the legislators had to submit to the legal principle that they had themselves invented and the rights of homosexuals became enshrined in law.

---

[36] *The New Encyclopaedia Britannica,* vol. 3, p. 339.

Unfortunately, that is only the beginning. In Sweden, the principle of consenting adults was used a number of years back to decriminalise incest. Consequently, it is legally permissible there for a man to have sexual relations with his mother, sister or daughter as long as they are consenting adults.

Islamic civilisation, on the other hand, regards the laws revealed by God as absolute and unchangeable. What was defined by God as morally evil one thousand four hundred years ago cannot ever become morally good because the fundamental nature of human beings and their societies has not and will never change. Without a solid moral foundation, human society will become corrupt. And leaving it up to humans to develop that foundation is inherently flawed. Allāh states in the Qur'ān: "If the truth were according to their desires, the heavens, the earth and all within them would be corrupted."[37] No matter what 'scientific' evidence is brought to prove that homosexuality is genetically or biologically based, it will still be considered a crime in the same way that adultery and fornication are considered crimes in spite of human inclination to it. Islām holds that sane adult human beings are still responsible for their choices. They are not robots, incapable of going beyond their programming. Some scientists are currently claiming that even crimes like robbery and murder have genetic origins. The question which remains is: If scientists also prove that paedophilia and rape are genetically based, will Western society also decriminalise them and do away with their rational principle of "consenting adults"?

Islamic law does not deny the role of society in formulating some of its laws. However, these laws are secondary or tertiary laws and not primary laws. There is a limited role for democracy in the Islamic principle of consultation stated in the Qur'ān: "Their affairs should be by mutual consultation."[38] For example, people

---

[37] Sūrah *al-Mu'minūn* (23):71.

[38] Sūrah *al-Shūra* (42):38.

in a community can decide by majority opinion to erect a traffic signal at a busy intersection where a number of traffic accidents have occurred. And later they may decide to remove it and make an underpass based on the same principle.

Western civilisation's total commitment to *secularism* even at the expense of *democracy* explains why the West strongly supports military dictatorships in Turkey and Algeria. Women in Turkey are prohibited from wearing scarves in any government institution, whether educational or political. When Merve Sefa Kavakci, a Member of Parliament recently challenged this law by showing up in the assembly wearing a scarf to take her parliamentary oath, she was forcibly removed and her Turkish citizenship was subsequently revoked. The right to wear a scarf publicly is defended in the West under the "freedom of religion" democratic policy, yet the West tolerates Turkish repression primarily because of Turkey's commitment to secularism. On the other hand, the West turned a blind eye when the Algerian military cancelled the results of free elections in order to stop the F.I.S. (The Islamic Party) from setting up an Islamic government through democratic elections which they were poised to win. Though the West stresses the importance of democracy, secularism is more important.

As to Chinese and Indian civilisations, both of which have a billion people within them, they have both succumbed to Western civilisation. When China embraced communism under the guidance of Chairman Mao Tse Tung, they embraced secular democracy. Communism was only an alternative economic experiment to capitalism. Its fundamental thought, as propounded by Marx, Lenin, etc., was secular democracy. The rule of the proletariat, the working masses, who constituted the majority of citizens, was supposed to be democratic. The Communist party ruled in the name of the proletariat, though not actually in their interests. Also, communist countries were even more anti-religion than capitalist ones. Atheism became the new state religion and other religions were systematically eliminated.

India, on the other hand, with a Muslim minority of over 100 million, chose secular democracy in order to avoid internal turmoil. At any rate, Hinduism is so much a conflicting mixture of cults and religions that it has no socio-economic system to offer. Hindu nationalism, as currently embodied in the BJP, is merely an assertion of Hinduism as a cultural identity. Its supporters argue that Muslims were originally Hindus and they should return to their religious roots.

Consequently, only Islām has a real alternative to Western civilisation and culture. Although the foundations of Islamic civilisation are clearly in direct conflict with those of Western civilisation, it does not mean that there are no common grounds. There remain many areas of good achieved by the West which Islamic civilisation can benefit from as Western civilisation benefited from the achievements of Muslims in the past.

Cultural Islām: Traditionalism

Although the West recognises Islām as the only civilisation capable of opposing its dominance, the Muslim world today is incapable of meeting the challenge. Western civilisation has succeeded in completely dominating the Muslim world and the little opposition that exists is systematically being stamped out. Consequently, Islamic civilisation is not being presented to the world as an alternative to Western civilisation. The important role that Allāh ascribed to the Muslim Nation is not being fulfilled. Allāh states in the Qur'ān: "You are the best nation extracted from among humankind because you command good, prohibit evil and you believe in Allāh."[39] The main reason for the current failure of Muslims to meet the challenge is due to the adulteration of Islamic teachings throughout the Muslim world today. Islamic practices have become so mixed with a variety of local customs and traditions that the average Muslim is unable to distinguish between what is Islām and what is, in fact, local culture.

The Islām being practised in much of the Muslim world today may be referred to as Cultural Islām or Folk Islām (as Christian missionaries like to refer to it). The main feature of this version of Islām is the blind following of local traditions. The existing cultures are generally a product of practices handed down from earlier generations. Some cultural practices are based on authentic Islamic traditions, while many are not. However, the cultural Muslim is unable to distinguish between the two. All traditions are

---

[39] Sūrah *Āl 'Imrān* (3):10.

identified as Islamic and any attempt to exclude any aspect of the cultural traditions is met with stiff resistance.

Although it is well known to all Muslims that Islām is based on the Qur'ān and the Sunnah,[40] when cultural Muslims are advised to follow instructions from the Qur'ān or the Sunnah they immediately make excuses for why they cannot. The excuses usually consist of statements to the effect that Islām was not practised that way in their village or country. Cultural Muslims are brainwashed with this response. Whenever they questioned a practice while growing up, their parents would scold them for questioning their traditions saying, "If it was good enough for our forefathers, it is good enough for you," or, "Do you think our forefathers were all wrong?" This response is very similar to that of the Makkan pagans when a similar invitation was given to them. God states in the Qur'ān:

وَإِذَا قِيلَ لَهُمْ تَعَالَوْاْ إِلَىٰ مَآ أَنزَلَ ٱللَّهُ وَإِلَى ٱلرَّسُولِ قَالُواْ
حَسْبُنَا مَا وَجَدْنَا عَلَيْهِ ءَابَآءَنَآ ۚ أَوَلَوْ كَانَ ءَابَآؤُهُمْ لَا يَعْلَمُونَ
شَيْـًٔا وَلَا يَهْتَدُونَ ﴿١٠٤﴾

> If you tell them, "Come to what Allāh has revealed and to the Messenger," they will reply, "What we found our parents doing is sufficient for us." Even though their parents knew nothing, nor were they rightly guided. Sūrah *al-Mā'idah* (5): 104.

In order for Muslims to re-establish Islamic civilisation and promote its ideals to the world as an alternative to Western culture, the inherited excess baggage of cultural Islām must be eliminated. Only pure unadulterated Islām can stand in the face of Western civilisation's cultural onslaught.

---

[40] The recorded life-style of Prophet Muḥammad consisting of his verbal instructions, his actions and actions of others approved by him.

There are four basic sources for un-Islamic traditions in Cultural Islām: Pre-Islamic practices, adopted practices, religious innovation and factionalism.

1. Pre-Islamic Practices

When Islām spread to various parts of the world, people who embraced the faith brought into Islām some of their pre-Islamic traditions. Islamic law did not prohibit all of the practices of the people whom it governed. A special category of law called *'urf* made allowances for local customs. Consequently, local traditions were permitted as long as they did not contradict clear commandments in the religion. The amount of un-Islamic customs which were carried into Islām by the new converts depended on the degree to which they learned Islām and the knowledge of those who invited them to Islām. The more ignorant they were of Islamic teachings, the easier it was for them to continue in their pre-Islamic habits. Likewise, those who taught the new converts would tolerate un-Islamic habits which they were ignorant of. For example, the red wedding dress of most Pakistani and Indian Muslims is identical to the Hindu wedding dress. There is no specified colour for the wedding dress according to Islamic law. It can be any colour, as long as it is not an imitation of the religious ceremonies of other religions. Consequently, white commonly used by Christians and red by Hindus should not be used.

These inherited practices might seem innocent and harmless in themselves. However, there are other inherited practices that are quite harmful physically as well as spiritually. For example, the pharaonic circumcision of females (genital mutilation) as practised in East Africa, the Sudan and Egypt among Muslims and non-Muslim tribes of that region is another example of inherited un-Islamic practices. It is harmful to women in that infections from it can lead to sterility and even death. And even under hospital supervision, it robs the woman of some if not all of her right to enjoy a basic part of her marriage. Furthermore, under the feminist attack, some women reject Islām under the mistaken impression that it condones this form of oppressive disfigurement of women.

Another example can be found in the inherited Hindu-European customs of dowry, wherein the family of the bride gives wealth and gifts to the groom. This has resulted in the phenomenon of bride-burning among Hindus in India. In response to this, the Indian government officially outlawed dowry. However, hundreds of Hindu women continue to be set on fire by their husbands annually in India as a result of their families not giving the gifts they promised at the time of marriage.

Woman burnt to death

Dhaka. A greedy husband burned to death his young wife at Shikpara in the city following a feud over dowry, police said. They said Zahir Mia poured kerosene over the body of his wife Shahnaj (20) and set fire to her on Sunday. She died at Dhaka Medical College Hospital yesterday.[41]

In Islām, the *mahr* (dowry) is supposed to be given by the groom to the bride as a symbol of his preparedness to look after her. However, in the Indian subcontinent, most Muslims have retained the Hindu practice of giving the dowry to the husband. As a result, the vicious criminal act of bride-burning, though less frequent, can be found among Muslims of that region also.

Domestic violence on rise in Pakistan

At least 300 women are burnt to death every year-report

Islamabad (Reuters)

A report by the private Pro-gressive Women's Association ... said that domestic violence in

[41] *Gulf News*, 28.2.98, p. 18, vol. 20, no. 139.

Pakistan was largely ignored and that proper legislation was needed to fight a rise in crimes against women. ...

"According to the associa-tions' findings, 'bride-burning' every year accounts for the violent death of at least 300 women, perpetrated most often by the victims' husbands or husband's families," said asso-ciation official Shamoon Hashmi.

In most of the cases the husbands or husband's families report to the police that the burning was an accident caused by an exploding stove and thus no prosecution takes place.

... The report gives graphic details and pictures of at least 12 women who were doused in kerosene and burnt by their close relatives and whose legal cases were pursued by the association but with most ending without any punishment to the suspects.[42]

In Southern Egypt, the custom among Muslims is that a widowed woman should not remarry. Some Southern Egyptians feel so strongly about this custom that they are prepared to commit murder in its defence.

Son held for killing mother

Qena, Egypt. A 22-year-old son beheaded and dismembered his widowed mother when he found out that she had secretly remarried, breaking with tradition in Southern Egypt, police here said yesterday. Salah A'mad Hassan, helped by one of his uncles, forced Samria Salam, 35, into the village cemetery in Naqada, a hamlet north of the southern resort of Luxor, where they strangled, beheaded and dismembered the woman, police said. They said the woman was pregnant. Hassan and Samria's brother were detained for questioning and admitted their crime.[43]

---

[42] *Gulf News*, 28.08.99, p. 18.

[43] *Gulf News*, 3.5.98, vol. 20, no. 202, p. 8.

The origin of this tradition can be found in ancient Egyptian mythology concerning the goddess Isis. According to the myths, Seth desired his sister, Isis, so much that he killed her husband, Osiris[44] in order to marry her. However, Isis refused to marry Seth and hid her son Horus until he came of age and revenged his father's death by killing his uncle, Seth. The cult of Isis began in Lower Egypt and spread throughout the whole country.[45]

Prohibiting widows from remarriage is fundamentally against Islamic teachings, which encourages marriage of widows and divorcees. In fact, most of Prophet Muḥammad's wives were widows.

2. Adopted Practices

Sometimes people borrowed practices from neighbouring un-Islamic states. For example, the celebration of the Prophet's birthday which was introduced almost 400 years after the time of the Prophet in the Fāṭimid Shi'ite state in Egypt. This celebration is in imitation of Christmas among Christians. During the *Mawlid* celebrations, music is often played and accompanied by dancing. Poems are sung in praise of the Prophet (ﷺ) often containing verses in which some of Allāh's attributes are given to the Prophet (ﷺ). For example, the most popular poem for *Mawlids* is that of *Qaṣīdah al-Burda* (The Ode of the Cloak) and is filled with *shirk*.

[44] The god of fertility and the personification of the dead king. This dual role was combined with the Egyptian dogma of divine kingship: the king at death became Osiris, god of the underworld; the dead king's son, the living king, was identified with Horus, god of the sky. (*The New Encyclopaedia Britannica,* vol. 8, p. 1026).

[45] Because she protected her son, she became the goddess of protection. As a mourner for her husband, she became the principal deity in all rites connected with the dead; as enchantress, she cured the sick and brought the dead to life; and as mother, she was herself a life-giver. (*The New Encyclopaedia Britannica,* vol. 6, p. 408).

Another example can be found in the practice of building tombs over graves. This tradition has become so popular that mausoleums like the Taj Mahal[46] have become modern cultural symbols of Islām. The evil of such a practice has been to turn some graves into places of worship. Shrines can be found all over the Muslim world and the masses of ignorant Muslims flock to them to perform worship in their vicinity and to ask favours from the dead. A classical example is that of the shrine of Shaykh Muʿīn ud-Dīn Chishti (d.1236), in Ajmer, Rajasthan state, northwestern India.[47] This shrine is the centre of pilgrimage for Muslims in the Indian subcontinent. While devotees (including Hindus) visit the white marble tomb complex in Ajmer throughout the year, the chief occasion for pilgrimage is the anniversary of Muʿīn al-Dīn's death, a festival known as the *'urs*.[48] The goal of pilgrimage is the mausoleum of Muʿīn ud-Dīn. Once the pilgrims reach the inner sanctum of the shrine, they bow low and kiss the tomb. Prayers are offered in thanksgiving for favours received, and petitions made for favours required. The prayers are in the form of oaths to give offerings to the shrine if prayers are answered. Devotees tie strings to the pierced-marble screens that surround parts of the mausoleum. These strings are removed when the prayers have been answered and offerings submitted. The devotees scatter red rose-petals over the tomb, and the privileged are given petals which have been lying there to keep as *ṭabarruḳ* or to eat. Pilgrims

[46] Built by the Moghul emperor, Shah Jahan in memory of his wife Mumtaz Mahal in Agra, India, in 1649. The entire complex took 20,000 workmen employed daily for 22 years to complete, at a cost of 40 million rupees. *The New Encyclopaedia Britannica,* vol. 2, p. 513.

[47] *The New Encyclopaedia Britannica,* vol. 1, p. 183.

[48] ʿUrs was originally used for marriage festivities, as opposed to *niḳāh*, the marriage ceremony. However, it was later used to refer to the ceremonies observed at the anniversary of the death of any celebrated saint. *Dictionary of Islam*, p. 655.

also spend time circumambulating the mausoleum, and sitting in its vicinity in passive and receptive silence to absorb the spiritual presence of the saint.[49]

Under colonial influence, Christian religious practices like wedding and engagement rings spread among Muslims. Today, most Muslims believe that it is a part of Islamic tradition. However, as was demonstrated in the marriage of Princess Diana which was televised internationally, the wedding ring is a symbol of trinitarian belief.

3. Religious Innovation [Ṣūfism]

Mysticism[50] is defined as an experience of union with God and the belief that man's main goal lies in seeking that union. The origins of mysticism can be found in the writings of ancient Greek philosophers like that of *Plato's Symposium* in which mention is made of various ladders of ascent, composed of steep and hard steps, whereby a union of the soul with God is finally attained.[51] A parallel concept can also be found in Hinduism's identification of *Atman* (human soul) with *Brahman* (the impersonal Absolute), the realisation of which is the ultimate goal or release from existence and rebirth.[52]

The mystic tradition kept alive in monastic Christianity began to find expression among Muslims from about 8th century CE, a century after the borders of the Islamic state had expanded to

---

[49] *The Shrine and Cult of Mu'in al-Din Chishti of Ajmer*, pp. 117-120.

[50] From the Greek "*Mystes*" meaning "one initiated into the mysteries." The term is derived from the Greek mystery religions whose initiates bore the name *"mystes" (Dictionary of Philosophy and Religion*, p. 374).

[51] *Colliers Encyclopedia*, vol. 17, p. 114.

[52] *Dictionary of Religions*, p. 68.

include Egypt and Syria and its major centers of monasticism.[53] A group of Muslims who were not satisfied with what the *Sharīʿah* (Islamic Law) had to offer, developed a parallel system which they named the *Ṭarīqah* (the way). Just as the ultimate goal of the Hindu was unity with the world soul and of the Christian mystic union with God; the ultimate goal of this movement became *Fanā*, the dissolution of the ego, and *Wuṣūl*, the meeting and unification of the human soul with Allāh in this life. A series of preliminary stages and states which had to be attained were defined. They were called *Maqāmāt* (stations) and *Ḥālāt* (states). A system of spiritual exercises was also designed for the initiate in order to bring about this "meeting." These exercises of *Dhikr*[54] often involved head and body movements and sometimes even dance, as in the case of whirling dervishes. All of these practices were attributed to the Prophet (ﷺ) through chains of narration in order to validate them, but there does not exist any authentic support for them in any of the classical books of Ḥadith. A multiplicity of systems evolved, and orders, similar to those among Christian monks, appeared named after their founders, like the *Qādiri, Chishti, Nakhshabandi,* and *Tījāni* orders. Along with that, volumes of legends and

---

[53] The authors of treatises on Muslim mysticism have often compared the "annihilation" of *Ṣūfism* with Buddhist *Nirvana*; but according to others this comparison is entirely inadequate as the Buddhist idea of annihilation is independent of the idea of God and includes the idea of transmigration of souls, to which *Nirvana* puts an end. In Muslim mysticism on the other hand, there is no question of the passing of the soul upon death into another body and the notion of a personal and all-present God is throughout predominant. The origin of the Muslim conception of *Fanā* has rather to be sought in Christianity from which it seems to be borrowed. This conception simply means the annihilation of the individual human will before the will of God, an idea which forms the centre of all Christian mysticism." (*Shorter Encyclopedia of Islam*, p. 98).

[54] *Dhikr*, which normally means the remembrance of God, is used to refer to the continuous repetition of God's names and attributes, in mystic circles.

fairy tales were spun around the founders and the outstanding personalities of these orders. And, just as Christian and Hindu monks chose special isolated structures (i.e. monasteries) in which to house their communities, the *Ṣūfī* orders developed similar housing schemes called *Zāwiyahs* (lit. corners).

In time, a body of heretic creeds developed out of the mystic "union-with-God" belief. For example, most orders claimed that Allāh could be seen when the state of *Wuṣūl* (arrival) was achieved. Yet when ʿĀ'ishah (ﷺ) asked the Prophet (ﷺ) if he saw Allāh during *Miʿrāj* (ascension), he replied that he had not.[55] Prophet Mūsā was also shown that neither he nor any man could withstand seeing Allāh in this life by Allāh revealing some of His being to a mountain which crumbled to dust during the revelation.[56] Some *Sūfī* adepts claimed that when the state of *Wuṣūl* was attained, the mundane obligations of *Sharīʿah* like five times daily *Ṣalāh*, were no longer obligatory. Most of them prescribed that prayers to Allāh could be sent through the Prophet (ﷺ) or through the so-called saints; many also began the practice of making *Ṭawāf*,[57] animal sacrifices and other acts of worship around the shrines and tombs of the saints. *Ṭawāf* can be observed today around the grave of Zaynab and Sayyid al-Badawī in Egypt, around the tomb of Muḥammad Aḥmad (The *Mahdi*) in Sudan, and around the Dargahs of countless saints and holy men in India and Pakistan, like that of Muʿin al-Dīn Chisti in Ajmer.

Music was introduced in most mystic circles and drugs like marijuana found its way into others as a means of heightening the pseudo-spiritual experience which they all sought. Such was the legacy of the latter generation of *Ṣūfīs* which had been built on the false premise that union of the human soul with Allāh was

---

[55] *Ṣaḥīḥ Muslim*, vol. 1, pp. 111-112, nos. 337, 339 and p. 113, no. 341.

[56] Sūrah *al-ʿA'rāf* (7):143.

[57] Walking around an object of religious devotion.

attainable. The early generation of pious individuals, like ʿAbdul-Qādir al-Jīlāni, and others to whom some orders were attributed, clearly understood the importance of distinguishing between the Creator and the created. The two could never become one, as One was Divine and Eternal, while the other was human and finite.

Perhaps the greatest harm resulting from mysticism is the introduction of intermediaries between God and humankind. Those who claimed the status of having become one with Allāh were elevated to "sainthood" and were either directly addressed in prayers or used as intercessors to God.

4. Religious Fanaticism or Factionalism

There are four main schools of Islamic jurisprudence (*madh-hab*)[58] followed by the majority of Muslims today. In modern times, they have become rallying points for the defenders of cultural Islām. In order to understand the divisive role played by the schools of Islamic law, one must first understand what is meant by the term "Islamic law" itself. The Arabic terms *Fiqh* and *Sharīʿah* have both been loosely translated into English as "Islamic Law", however, these terms are not synonymous either in the Arabic language or to the Muslim scholar.

Sharīʿah, literally means 'a waterhole where animals gather daily to drink', or 'the straight path' as in the Qur'ānic verse:

ثُمَّ جَعَلْنَٰكَ عَلَىٰ شَرِيعَةٍ مِّنَ ٱلْأَمْرِ فَٱتَّبِعْهَا وَلَا تَتَّبِعْ
أَهْوَآءَ ٱلَّذِينَ لَا يَعْلَمُونَ ﴿١٨﴾

> "Then We put you on a straight path (*Sharīʿah*) in your affairs, so follow it and do not follow the desires of those who have no knowledge." Sūrah *al-Jāthiya* (45):18.

---

[58] The names of the schools are *Ḥanafī, Shāfiʿī, Mālikī* and *Ḥanbalī.*

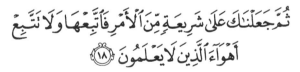

Islamically, *Sharī'ah* refers to the sum total of Islamic laws which were revealed to Prophet Muḥammad (ﷺ) and recorded in the Qur'ān as well as deducible from the Prophet's divinely guided lifestyle called the sunnah.

Fiqh literally means, the true understanding of what is intended. An example of this usage can be found in the Prophet Muḥammad's statement: *"To whomsoever Allāh wishes good, He gives the Fiqh (true understanding) of the religion."*[59] Technically, however, *Fiqh* refers to 'the science of deducing Islamic laws from evidence found in the sources of Islamic law'. The main tool of *Fiqh* is *Ijtihād* (reasoned ruling) which operates through *Ijmā* (consensus) and *Qiyās* (deduction by analogy). By extension, the term *Fiqh* has also come to mean the body of deduced Islamic laws.

The Distinction

From the previous two definitions, the following three differences may be deduced:

1. *Sharī'ah* is the body of revealed laws found in both the Qur'ān and the sunnah, while *Fiqh* is the body of laws deduced from *Sharī'ah* to cover specific situations not directly treated in *Sharī'ah law.*
2. *Sharī'ah* is fixed and unchangeable, whereas *Fiqh* changes according to the circumstances under which it is applied.
3. The laws of *Sharī'ah* are, for the most part, general: they lay down basic principles. In contrast, the laws of *Fiqh* tend to be specific: they demonstrate how the

[59] *Ṣaḥīḥ al Bukhāri*, vol. 4, pp. 223-4, no. 346 and *Ṣaḥīḥ Muslim,* vol. 3, p. 1061, no. 4720.

basic principles of *Sharīʿah* should be applied in given circumstances.[60]

The significance of the distinction between *Fiqh* and *Sharīʿah* lies in the relevance of Islamic law to all times. Most people find it hard to understand how laws revealed 1,400 years ago could be relevant to human society today, especially when they consider the laws of Europe in the Dark and Middle Ages and the feudal societies which have since been abolished. Islamic laws address the basic instincts of human beings and their relationships with God, other humans and the world in which they live. Human nature, in the Islamic view, has not changed, nor will it ever change. Changes in technology have not made human beings morally superior. In fact, modern societies are far more corrupt than those of the past. Furthermore, modern technology should not be looked at as being superior in all respects to the past, because there are technologies of the ancients that continue to defy modern knowledge until today. Examples of this include the mummification processes used by the ancient Egyptians and the building of their pyramids, or the ability of ancient Mayans of Central America to polish pieces of metal into mirrors using only the crudest implements of their times. Consequently, the laws outlined in revelation remain as pertinent to humans today as they did at the time of their revelation. The *Fiqh* component of Islamic law adds the necessary flexibility for the application of the divine laws to all new circumstances.

The Islamic Renaissance

All the *madh-habs* contributed in different degrees to the development of *Fiqh* and no single *madh-hab* can properly be claimed to represent Islām or Islamic law in its totality. All of the schools have been important instruments for the clarification

---

[60] *The Evolution of Fiqh,* pp. 1-2.

and application of the *Sharī'ah*. In fact, the only infallible *madh-hab* which deserves to be followed without question is that of Prophet Muḥammad (ﷺ) himself. Only his interpretations of the *Sharī'ah* can rightly be considered divinely guided and meant to be followed until the last day of this world. All other *madh-habs* are a product of human effort, and are therefore subject to human error. Or as Imām al-Shāfi'i, founder of the Shāfi'i *madh-hab*, so wisely put it, "There aren't any of us who haven't had a saying or action of Allāh's Messenger (ﷺ) elude him or slip his mind. So, no matter what rulings I have made or fundamental principles I have established, there will be in them things contrary to the way of Allāh's Messenger (ﷺ). However, the correct ruling is according to what the Messenger of Allāh (ﷺ) said, and that is my true ruling."[61]

Evolution of the *Madh-habs*

In the era of the Righteous Caliphs, the *Fiqh* principle of *Ijmā* (decisions by unanimity) evolved and *ijtihād* (reasoned rulings) became an independent principle of *Fiqh* under the name of *Qiyās*. The *madh-hab* during this period was, in reality, that of each of the Righteous Caliphs, since the final say in legal matters rested with them. However, all legal decisions were subject to alteration on the basis of recorded statements or practices of the Prophet (ﷺ), i.e. *ḥadīths*.

During the 'Umayyad dynasty (661-750 CE), there was a shift from caliphate to monarchy and the caliph/king was no longer the head of the *madh-hab*. Scholars among the companions of the Prophet (ﷺ) and their students left the centers of the Islamic state and dispersed in the outer lying provinces. This led to an increase

[61] Collected by al-Ḥākim, Ibn 'Asākir, *Tārīkh Dimishq,* vol. 15, sec. 1, p. 3.

in *ijtihād* as *Ijmā* became increasingly difficult to achieve. During this period, students of *Fiqh* freely and frequently changed teachers and exchanged legal opinions. In the first hundred years of the 'Abbāside dynasty (750-850 CE), many *madh-habs* flourished and though they were becoming distinct entities, they maintained the characteristic of flexibility in making and accepting legal rulings which existed in the previous period. Besides the current four, the Awzā'ī, Laythī, Thawrī, Ẓāhirī and Jarīrī *madh-habs* were among the well-known *madh-habs* of this period. Following the deaths of the major scholars, the *madh-habs* rigidity began to set in. During the latter period of the 'Abbāsid dynasty, between the year 950 CE and the sacking of Baghdad (1258 CE), court debates (called *Munātharāt*) between scholars of different *madh-habs* for the entertainment of the caliphs and their entourage became popular. This spawned competitiveness and dogmatism, since the loss of a debate not only meant the loss of monetary reward from the caliph but it also meant the loss of personal prestige and that of one's *madh-hab*. Consequently, the principle of defending one's *madh-hab* right or wrong came to be considered a virtue. As a result, *madh-hab* sectarianism and fanaticism became rampant among the court scholars. In time, the spirit of rivalry largely generated by these debates spread to the masses, and *madh-hab* factionalism became widespread.[62]

Four *Madh-habs*

During this stage, the number of major *madh-habs* dwindled to four; three major and one minor. In other words, the *madh-habs* of great Imāms like al-Awzā'ī, Sufyān al-Thawrī, Ibn Abī Laylā, Abū Thawr and al-Layth ibn Sa'd had all disappeared leaving only

[62] *Al-Madkhal,* pp. 147-57.

the *madh-habs* of Abū Ḥanīfah, Mālik, al-Shāfiʿī and Aḥmad ibn Ḥanbal. In time, these schools of Islamic legal thought became so predominant that the common people soon forgot that any other school ever existed. Furthermore, each of these schools took on a dynamic of its own and their followers started the practice of naming themselves after their respective *madh-habs*. For example, al-Ḥuṣayn ibn Masʿūd al-Baghawī, author of the *Fiqh* classic, *Sharḥ al-Sunnah*, was commonly referred to as al-Ḥusayn ibn Masʿūd al-Baghawī al-Shāfiʿī after the Shāfiʿī *madh-hab*.

Emergence of *Taqlīd*[63]

The six centuries starting with the sacking of Baghdad in 1258 CE and the execution of the last ʿAbbāsid caliph, al-Mustaʿṣim, and ending around the middle of the nineteenth century of the Christian era may be referred to as the "Muslim Dark Ages." It represents the rise of the Ottoman Empire, founded in 1299 CE by the Turkish leader ʿUthmān I, until its decline under the attacks of European colonialism.

Scholars of this period left all forms of *Ijtihād* and unanimously issued a legal ruling which was intended to close the door of *Ijtihād* permanently. They reasoned that all possible issues had already been raised and addressed, and there was therefore no need for further *Ijtihād*.[64] With this step, a new concept of *madh-hab* arose, namely that one of the four *madh-habs* had to be followed for one's Islām to be valid. In time, this concept became firmly embedded among the masses as well as the scholars of *Fiqh*. Consequently, the religion of Islām itself became restricted within the confines of

---

[63] The blind following of a *Madh-hab*.

[64] Muḥammad Ḥusayn al-Dhahabī, *al-Sharīʿah al-Islāmīyah,* (Egypt: Dār al-Kutub al-Ḥadīth, 2nd ed.1968), p. 12.

the four existing *madh-habs*; Ḥanafī, Mālikī, Shāfiʿī and Ḥanbalī. These schools of law came to be considered divinely ordained manifestations of Islām. It was claimed that all of them were completely correct, equal and representative of true Islām, yet there were innumerable differences among them. In fact, there were scholars in this period who interpreted some *Ḥadīths* in such a way as to prove that the Prophet (ﷺ) himself had predicted the appearance of the Imāms and their *madh-habs*. Consequently, any attempt to go beyond these canonical *madh-habs* was considered heretical and anyone who refused to follow one of them was classified an apostate. The hyper conservative scholars of this stage even went so far as to rule that whoever was caught transferring from one *madh-hab* to another was liable to punishment at the discretion of the local judge. A ruling was also made in the Ḥanafī *madh-hab* prohibiting the marriage of a Ḥanafī to a Shāfiʿī.[65] And even the second most important pillar of Islām, *Ṣalāh*, was not spared the effects of *madh-hab* fanaticism. The followers of the various *madh-habs* began to refuse to pray behind Imāms from other *madh-habs*. This resulted in the building of separate prayer niches in the masjids[66] of communities where more than one *madh-hab* existed. Even the most holy masjid, *Al-Masjid Al-Ḥarām* of Makkah, which represents the unity of Muslims and the religion of Islām, was affected. Separate prayer niches were set up around the Kaʿbah: one for an Imām from each of the schools. And when the time for *Ṣalāh* came, an Imām from one of the *madh-habs* would lead a congregation of followers from his *madh-hab* in prayer; then another Imām from one of the other *madh-habs* would lead his congregation of followers and so on. Separate places of prayer for each of the *madh-hab* remained around the Kaʿbah until the first

---

[65] Muḥammad Nāṣir al-Dīn al-Albānī, *Ṣifah Ṣalāh al-Nabī*, (Beirut: al-Maktab al-Islāmī ninth ed. 1972), p. 51.

[66] *Masjid* (plural *Masājid*), the Muslim house of worship.

quarter of the twentieth century when ʿAbdul-ʿAzīz ibn Saʿūd and his army conquered Makkah in 1924 and united all worshippers behind a single Imām regardless of his or their *madh-habs*.

During this period, some books on the fundamentals of *Fiqh (Usūl al-Fiqh)* were written. In these works, the correct method of making *Ijtihād* was outlined and the conditions for its application were clearly defined. However, the conditions which were laid down by these scholars were so strict that they excluded not only the scholars of their time but also many of the earlier scholars who had made *Ijtihād*. There were also a few books which were written on comparative *Fiqh* during this period. As in the previous period, the opinions of the *madh-hab* and their proofs were collected and criticized in these books. The authors then defined as most accurate those opinions which were held by their particular *madh-hab*.

Toward the end of this period, an attempt was made to codify Islamic law under the auspices of the Ottoman caliphs. A panel of seven top ranking scholars of *Fiqh* was formed and entrusted with the job. It was completed in 1876 CE and enforced as law by the Sultan throughout the Ottoman empire under the title *Majallah al-Aḥkām al-ʿĀdilah* (The Just Codes).[67] However, even this seemingly noble attempt was affected by *madh-hab* fanaticism. All of the scholars on the committee were appointed from the Ḥanafi *madh-hab*. Consequently, the resulting code totally ignored the contribution of the other *madh-habs* to *Fiqh*.

With the expeditions of Columbus (1492) and Vasco de Gama in the 15th century, Western European states began to capture the routes and sources of international trade. Subsequently, Muslim East Asian states were absorbed by European imperialism beginning

---

[67] Anwar Aḥmed Qadri, *Islamic Jurisprudence in the Modern World,* (Lahore, Pakistan: Ashraf, First edition 1963) p. 65.

with Java which fell to the Dutch in 1684. After Transylvania and Hungary fell from Ottoman hands to Austria in 1699 and the defeat of the Ottomans by Russia in the Russo Turkish war of 1768-74, the European territories of the Ottoman empire were soon lost, one after another.[68] This process culminated in the total dissolution of the Ottoman Empire during the First World War and its division into colonies and protectorates. Consequently, European law codes replaced Islamic laws throughout the Muslim world.

Although European colonialism officially ended some years ago, Islamic law has remained in disuse in all Muslim countries with the exception of Saudi Arabia which has codified Islamic law according to the Ḥanbalī *madh-hab*, Pakistan to a large degree according to the Ḥanafī *madh-hab* and Iran which has recently done so according to the Ja'farī *madh-hab*.[69]

Reformers

In spite of the general decay described above, there existed throughout this period a number of outstanding scholars who opposed *Taqlīd* and dared to raise the banner of *Ijtihād*. They called for a return to the roots of the religion, to the true sources of Islamic law and to reliance on these foundations above all else. Foremost among them was Aḥmad ibn Taymiyyah (1263-1328 CE). Because of his challenge of the status quo, many of his contemporaries declared him an apostate and had the authorities jail him repeatedly. Ibn Taymiyyah was, however, one of the greatest scholars of his time. Initially, he had studied *Fiqh* according to the Ḥanbalī *madh-hab*, but did not restrict himself

---

[68] *Islamic Jurisprudence in the Modern World,* p. 85.

[69] The *Fiqh madh-hab* of the Ithnā 'Ashrīyah (Twelver) Shi'ite sect falsely attributed to Imām Ja'far al-Ṣādiq (d.765 CE).

to it. He studied the sources of Islamic law in depth and mastered all the Islamic sciences which were known at that time. Ibn Taymiyyah's students were among the greatest Islamic scholars of their time and carried on to the next generation the banner of *Ijtihād* and a return to the pure sources of Islām which he had raised. Among them was Ibn Qayyim (1292-1350), a great scholar in the fields of *Fiqh* and *Ḥadīth*, al-Dhahabī (1274-1348), a master in the science of *Ḥadīth* criticism and Ibn Kathīr (1302-1373), a master in *Tafsīr*, History and *Ḥadīth*.

Another noteworthy reformer was the great scholar Aḥmad ibn 'Abdur-Raḥīm better known as Shah Waliullāh Dihlawī (1703-1762 CE). He was born in the Indian sub-continent where *Taqlīd* was, perhaps, most rampant. After he had mastered the various Islamic sciences and Ḥanafī *Fiqh*, he called for the re-opening of the door of *Ijtihād* and the re-unification of the schools of *Fiqh*. In his efforts to re-examine Islamic principles and to find out on what authority the legal schools based their regulations, Shah Waliullāh rejuvenated the study of *Ḥadīth*. Although he did not go so far as to reject the existing *Fiqh* schools, he did teach that everyone was free to choose a particular decision different from that taken by the school to which he belonged himself, if he was convinced that the case was better confirmed by *Ḥadīth*.[70]

Muḥammad ibn 'Alī al-Shawkānī (1757-1835 CE) born near the town of Shawkān in Yemen, was also among the reformers of this period. Al-Shawkānī studied *Fiqh* according to the Zaydī *madh-hab*[71] and became one of its outstanding scholars. He then went into an in-depth study of the science of *Ḥadīth* and subsequently became the most famous scholar of *Ḥadīth* of his time. At this point, he freed himself from the confines of the *madh-*

---

[70] A.J. Arberry, *Religion in the Middle East* (Cambridge University Press, 1969-reprinted 1981) vol. 2, pp. 128-9.

[71] One of the major *Shi'ite Madh-habs* of *Fiqh* (see pp. 60-65).

hab and began making independent *Ijtihād*. He wrote a number of works in *Fiqh* and its fundamentals in which issues studied from the points of view of all the *madh-habs* were concluded with solutions based solely on the most accurate proofs and the most convincing arguments. Imām al-Shawkānī took the position that *Taqlīd* was *Ḥarām* and wrote a number of books on the topic. Consequently, he also came under attack from most of the scholars of his time.[72]

The Islamic Renaissance

In the nineteenth century, Muslim intellectuals openly rebelled against Cultural Islām. Their revolt produced two major philosophical trends: modernism and fundamentalism.

1) Modernism was the Westernized-Muslim response to Cultural Islām. It was noted for its so-called "rationalist" approach. The modernist reaction sought to modify Islamic teachings in order to make it conform with Western culture.

2) The orthodox response '*madh-hab* fanaticism' could be termed Fundamentalism, meaning a return to the fundamentals of Islamic thought and civilisation. It was a call to the Qur'ān and Sunnah as the guiding light in Muslim affairs.

Modernism

The leader of this trend was Jamāl al-Dīn al-Afghānī (1839-1897 CE) who travelled throughout the Muslim world calling for reform and Pan-Islamism. Jamāl al-Dīn travelled to India,

---

[72] Muḥammad ibn 'Alī al-Shawkānī, *Nayl al-Awṭār,* vol. 1, pp. 3-6.

Makkah, and Constantinople, settling finally in Egypt. He called for free political, religious and scientific thought and denounced *Taqlīd* and state corruption. Jamāl al-Dīn taught these ideas at the University of al-'Azhar[73] and influenced many who studied under him. Unfortunately, some of Jamāl al-Dīn's ideas were extreme. For example, he elevated the human mind and its logical deductions to a level equal to that of Divine Revelation. His intentions also became suspect due to his involvement with the Masonic movement which was at that time establishing new branches in the Middle-East.[74]

Muḥammad 'Abduh (1849-1905 CE) was among Afghānī's most famous students. Under the influence of Afghānī and Ibn Taymiyyah's thought, the banner of *Ijtihād* was again raised high by Muḥammad 'Abduh, and *Taqlīd* and its supporters were systematically attacked. Afghānī had taught a revival of each Muslim nation internally as part of a general pan-Islamic movement in which the reviving nations were to co-operate. Shaykh 'Abduh concentrated his efforts on Egypt itself, and stressed immediate moral reforms, enlightened education, and careful reinterpretation of religious doctrine. But, the effects of Afghānī's extremist views caused Muḥammad 'Abduh to lean toward extreme modernism, and he also eventually deviated in some of his interpretations and legal rulings. For example, in his *Tafsīr* of the Qur'ān, 'Abduh apologetically explained away all of the miracles attributed to the prophets directly and performed by God through the forces of nature. To him the flocks of birds

---

[73] The oldest and most famous Islamic University in the Muslim world. It was first established in Egypt by the Fāṭimid Shi'ite state in the year 361 AH/972 CE.

[74] Muḥammad Muḥammad Ḥusayn, *al-Ittijāhāt al-Waṭanīyah fī al-Adab al-'Arabī al-Mu'āṣir,* vol. 1, p. 153. See also *Religion in the Middle East*, vol. 2, p. 37.

which dropped clay pebbles on the Yemenite army of Abrahah and his elephant during their attack on the Ka'bah, mentioned in the Qur'ān, were simply airborne microbes which spread disease among them. Likewise, he 'issued' *Fatāwā* allowing Muslims to be involved in business transactions involving interest. He based this ruling on the *Fiqh* principle that dire necessity makes the forbidden allowable. The fallacy of his ruling lay in the fact that *Fiqh* specially defines dire necessity as involving matters of life and death or loss of limb, and this was simply not the case where business transactions are concerned. Muḥammad 'Abduh's main student, Muḥammad Rashīd Riḍā (d. 1935), carried on his mentor's attack on *Taqlīd*, but rejected most of his teacher's excesses. However, other students of Muḥammad 'Abduh became the nucleus of the extreme modernist movement and deviated in many areas even more than their teacher. For example, his student Qāsim Amīn (d. 1908) was the first to make a vehement attack on polygamy, the simplicity of Islamic divorce and the use of the veil.

In India, Sir Sayyid Aḥmad Khan (1817-1898) proposed an overall program of Muslim revival on the basis of full co-operation with the British Colonialist administration. He sought to interpret Islām according to the Liberal nineteenth-century worldview most prominently presented in British culture. According to that worldview, the primary source of truth was natural-scientific inquiry, and the trend of human life was by nature an ever-expanding awareness of such scientific truth which would actualize human potentialities for good. The good life meant, above all, human prosperity and individual freedom. Aḥmad Khan taught that Islām was essentially the spirit of the Qur'ān, without later additions. In the spirit of the Qur'ān, he found an appeal to recognition of the natural world, an earthy sense of human well-being, and a strong activism. He called his doctrine by an Arabised English term, *nechariyyah,* naturalism, and offered it as a reform platform within Islam. However, his new theology was not widely received, and the '*ulamā* effectively tore apart his arguments.

His stress on the practical reasonableness of Islām was generally acceptable among the well to do Muslims. Consequently, they supported his foundation of the Anglo-Mohammedan Oriental College at Aligarh in 1875. The college taught on one hand the Muslim religion and on the other hand the modern European arts and sciences, the latter in English. Graduates of the college would be qualified to serve in British business firms or in the British governmental apparatus, while, in theory, remaining good Muslims.[75] Aligarh University later became a hot bed for communism and Islamic elements have remained weak on campus until the present.

The well-to-do Muslims also accepted Aḥmad Khan's political lead, which was to try to forge a special alliance between the British and the Muslim upper classes, founded on implicit loyalty to the British regime as the provider of Modern good order and enlightenment to India.

Some of his disciples worked out a less radical justification for such a policy, interpreting Islām, as basically Liberal; but seeing in the Islām of the classical ʿAbbāside caliphate, with its cultural openness and its fostering of science, a sufficient model for their present departure. They declared that science and progress had come to the West from Islām to begin with; that in the ages of Sūfism, Islām declined from its pristine progressiveness; and that what they must now do was recapture, as apprentices to the West, what Islam had meantime lost.[76]

Movements

In the beginning of the twentieth century, movements and groups arose calling to the return of Islamic rule in Muslim lands

---

[75] Ibid., pp. 334-336.

[76] Ibid., pp. 334-336.

and to the reformation of Muslim beliefs and practices. Among the political movements were those of Ḥasān al-Bannā (d. 1949), founder of the *Ikhwān Muslimūn* movement in Egypt and Sayyid, Abul-A'lā Mawdudi (1903-1979), founder of the Jamā'at Islāmi movement in India. Both of these movements called for the establishment of an Islamic state to replace the existing colonial or neo-colonial administrations. Consequently, they both came into conflict with the rulers of their areas. When Jamāl 'Abdun-Nāṣir seized control of the government, he systematically rounded up members of the movement and tortured and executed many of them in order to crush it. The *Ikhwān* was then forced underground, and became a secret society which developed a structure similar to communist cells in order to continue to operate. Oaths of allegiance were required of all members and the call Islamic State evolved into a recruitment drive for members. Very little efforts were made to correct beliefs and practices as collecting members became the chief priority. Controversial issues of beliefs and practices were seen as divisive and, as such, were deliberately avoided. Their members who fled to the West to avoid persecution and further their academic studies set up student organizations like F.O.S.I.S., M.S.A. and I.S.N.A. through which members continued to be recruited.

Another movement arose in India during this period which prided itself in being totally apolitical. Maulana Muḥammad Ilyas founded, what came to be known as the *Tablīgh* Movement. Its main focus was on bringing Muslims back to the mosques which had become empty over the years of Colonial rule. In order to appeal to the general masses, its founder combined the practices of the major Sūfi sects of the continent in its inner teachings. Travel to different locations to invite Muslims was added to its outer practices. Its apolitical stance has enabled it to spread to all corners of the Muslim world without resistance from Muslim or non-Muslim governments. However, very little effort is made to correct the beliefs and practices of its members and its main text, *Tablīghī Nisāb*, is filled with inauthentic material. The tradition of *Taqlīd* remained alive in all of these movements as avoiding it facilitated recruitment of followers.

Parallel to the previously mentioned movements, another set of movements evolved from the tradition of the earlier reformers who opposed *Taqlīd* and called to a return to the Qur'ān and Sunnah as they were understood by the Prophet's companions and the early generations of righteous scholars. These groups are generally referred to as the *Salafī* movements. In Egypt, the *Anṣār al-Sunnah* movement was founded by Shaykh Ḥāmid al-Fiqhī, 'Abdur-Raḥmān al-Wakīl and 'Abdur-Razzāq Ḥamzah and in India the *Ahl-e-Ḥadīth* movement was formally established by Shaykh Thanā'ullāh al-Amritsarī. The *Salafī* groups focused on the correction of Muslim beliefs and practices as a prerequisite for change. They opposed the factionalist attitudes which developed in the political movements as well as exhibiting a negative attitude towards knowledge and innovated practices which had developed in the *Tablīgh* movement. In the second half of the twentieth century, the great *Ḥadīth* scholar of our era, Nāṣir al-Dīn al-Albānī, picked up the banner of Islamic Revival in Syria as did Shaykh Ibn Bāz and Shaykh Ibn 'Uthaymīn in Saudi Arabia. In Yemen, one of Shaykh Nāṣir ud-Dīn's students, Shaykh Muqbil ibn Hādī continued the call to reform of beliefs and practices.

The ugly head of *hizbiyyah* (factionalism), which had plagued Muslims through the misinterpretation of the *madh-habs*, again reared its head in the political and apolitical movements of the twentieth century. These groups shared the common characteristic of fundamentally calling people to 'their' organization and to avoid others. They have ameers to whom the followers pledge oaths of allegiance which should only be given to the true leader of all Muslims. They all contain bits and pieces of what Muslims need, however, they are lacking the most fundamental component which is *'aqīdah* (correct beliefs). Muslims do need to revive Islamic government and the caliphate and they do need to get Muslims back to the mosques. But the focus must be on *'aqīdah*, first and foremost. Gathering for the sake of overthrowing foreign rule in Algeria in the Fifties did not bring Islamic rule into place because the communist elements among the Muslim forces hijacked the 'revolution'. In Afghanistan, Muslim groups came together to combat the threat of communism, but after Russian forces were expelled and the communist regime overthrown, the Muslim groups turned on each other. In Egypt, the *Ikhwān* have tried to resurface under a political cover, patiently trying to work their way in through the political process. However, the next generation of youths, due to their lack of knowledge and upbringing were no longer prepared to wait. As far as they were concerned, the Islamic revival was taking place in Iran; the Islamic state was being established now. Many from the *Ikhwān* gave oaths of allegiance to Khomeini as the caliph. New offshoots from the *Ikhwān* appeared under the names of *Takfīr wal-Hijrah, Jamā'at ul-Jihād,* and *al-Jamā'ah al-Islāmiyyah* with members prepared to seize power immediately. In these groups, a philosophy of violence evolved which was justified by declaring all Muslim rulers to be disbelievers as well as all those who worked in state institutions. The president of Egypt, Anwar Sadāt, was executed in the hope that Islamic rule could be forced upon the state. However, Sadāt's successor, Mubārak, was far more repressive against law-abiding members of the *Ikhwān* than Sadāt had ever been. The situation for Muslim activists became far worse as a result of the wave of violence unleashed by these new offshoots. Similarly in Syria, the *Ikhwān* tried to take over the government by revolting in the cities of Hams and Hama, expecting the masses of Muslims of Syria to come to their aid. However, even though the vast majority of the Syrians are Sunni Muslims, and the ruling class belonged to the extreme Shi'ite Nusayrite of Hafad Asād, they controlled the artillery, tanks, and planes. The Sunni Muslims were the foot soldiers. Consequently, when Ḥāfiẓ Asad's armoured battalions turned on the *Ikhwān* in Hams and Hama, they were swiftly wiped out. Furthermore, their cries for help to Iran, which had formerly considered the Nusayrites as apostates, outside the Shi'ite fold, went unheard. Instead, Khomeini officially welcomed Ḥāfiẓ Asad back into the Shi'ite fold as he slaughtered the *Ikhwān* activists and raped their women. In Algeria, the F.I.S. movement sought to reestablish Islām thought the democratic political process. However, the military government undermined it by canceling the elections and jailing the F.I.S. leadership. Consequently, as in Egypt before, the members went underground and its military wing began an urban guerilla struggle. In response, the government formed another group, the G.I.A. which committed atrocities in the name of the Islamic movement and alienated the masses from the legitimate struggle. Eventually, the F.I.S. was forced to renounce and abandon violent means in order to regain credibility among the masses. By not focusing on *'aqīdah* the movement engaged in a battle they were ill-equipped to win and which set it back many years.

"Fundamentalism"

During the last half of the twentieth century, all Muslim groups and movements, whether political, apolitical or *Salafī* came to be labelled as "fundamentalist" by Western press. However, this label included the terrorist practices of extremist political groups like the P.L.O. and extremist religious groups like the *Jihād* movement of Egypt. All Muslim groups came to be perceived by Western eyes as terrorist and violent.

In a television interview, Willi Claes, Secretary General of NATO, stated:

> "Muslim fundamentalism is at least as dangerous as communism once was. Please do not underestimate this risk … at the conclusion of this age it is a serious threat, because it represents terrorism, religious fanaticism and exploitation of social and economic justice."[77]

---

[77] Reported by Inter Press Service, 18 February 1995, quoted in *Islamophobia: a challenge for us all,* p. 9.

By definition, fundamentalism is a conservative Protestant theological movement based on belief in the verbal infallibility of the Bible. It developed in America, in the late 19th century as a reaction against the theory of evolution and the historical study of the Bible (Higher Criticism). It opposed liberal attempts to reconcile the teachings of Christianity with the findings of science.

According to this definition, every Muslim must be a fundamentalist, because all Muslims hold that the Qur'ān, the Muslim Scripture, is 100% the word of God. There are no Muslim scholars who question the Qur'ān's authenticity, and it is unanimously agreed among Muslim scholars past and present that anyone who denies even a word of the Qur'ān has become apostate from Islām.

The Solution

The only solution to the current dilemma facing Muslims is to return to the true roots of Islamic civilisation and culture. The way lies in rediscovering the correct sources of Islamic knowledge and the correct methodology of interpreting it. There is no other way. As Imām Mālik said, "The latter part of this nation will not be able to reform itself successfully except by using what reformed its early part." Prophet Muḥammad (ﷺ) informed his followers that the Muslim nation would split up into 73 different sects, 72 of which lead to hell and only one leading to paradise. Then, he clarified that the path to paradise was the path he was on and that his companions were on. That is what is known as the way of the *Salaf*. However, this methodology or *manhaj* is one which is not isolationist; one which abandons and boycotts all who make any mistakes along the way. As Shaykh Nāṣirud-Dīn himself stated in many of his lectures, abandonment (*ḥajr*) is not to be practised in these times as it will not achieve the goals it was originally intended for. In the past, isolation of one who practised innovation served to bring him or her back into the fold of correct Islām, as their deviation would appear obvious. However, in these times in which the mass of Muslims practise some form of deviation or another, boycotting only serves to isolate the few who are on the correct methodology. Consequently, the best method is that of patient advice and good treatment in order to open avenues for acceptance of change. As the Prophet (ﷺ) himself said, "*The religion consists essentially of good advice.*"

Islamic Culture

Islamic Culture represents the traditions and customs which evolve from the day-to-day practice of people following the authentic teachings of Islām. In general, when the various cultures of Muslims around the world are compared, the common features found in all countries and regions represent the core of Islamic culture, and the variations represent the basic features of Muslim cultures.

For example, the dress of Muslim women varies in colour, style and material according to Muslim culture. However, they all share the basic Islamic cultural principle of covering the whole body except for or including face and hands. Another example may be seen in the dress of Muslim men. In the past, Muslim men wore a variety of clothing, designs, and colours. However, their clothing all shared the basic Islamic cultural principles. They covered the area between the navel and knee with loose garments either in the form of baggy pants, a thobe (full length shirt), or a lungi / sarong (wrap around skirt), which did not hang below the ankle. They were also not made from silk nor were they the bright orange-yellow colour traditionally used by Buddhist monks. Today, the standard garment worn by men in most Muslim countries is the western pant that is deliberately designed to expose the private parts. Furthermore, it is worn hanging below the ankles.

The Foundation of Islām

The teachings of Islām are based on five fundamental principles called the five pillars of Islām, and six fundamental beliefs called the six pillars of Īmān (faith). This division is based on the following well-known tradition of the Prophet (ﷺ) called *ḥadīth Jibrīl*.

Abū Hurayrah related that on one occasion while they were sitting with the Messenger of Allāh, he said to them,

> "Ask me anything,"

but they were too overawed out of profound respect to ask him anything.[78] 'Umar ibn al-Khaṭṭāb [79] said,

> "While we were sitting with the Messenger of Allāh (ﷺ) a man came among us whose clothes were exceedingly white and whose hair was jet black. No signs of journeying were to be seen on him and none of us knew him. He walked up and sat down by the Prophet (ﷺ). Resting his knees against his and placing the palms of his hands on his thighs, he said: O Muḥammad, tell me about Islam. The Messenger of Allāh (ﷺ) said: Islam is to testify that there is no god but Allāh and Muḥammad is the Messenger of Allāh, to perform the prayers, to pay the *Zakāh*,[80] to fast in *Ramaḍān*, and to make the pilgrimage to the House[81] if you are able to do so. He said: You have spoken rightly, and we were amazed at him asking him and saying that he had spoken rightly. He said: Then tell me about *Īmān*.[82] He said: It is to believe in Allāh, His angels, His books, His messengers, and the Last Day, and to believe in divine destiny, both the good and the evil thereof. He said:

---

[78] *Ṣaḥīḥ Muslim,* vol. 1, pp. 4-5, no. 6.

[79] The second Caliph.

[80] Often rendered as "alms-tax" or "poor-due", it is a tax levied on a man's wealth and distributed among the poor.

[81] The Ka'bah and Mosque in Makkah.

[82] *Īmān* is generally rendered as "religious belief" or "faith". However, being a fundamental term in Islām, the Arabic word has been retained.

You have spoken rightly. He said: Then tell me about *iḥsān*.[83] He said: It is to worship Allāh as though you are seeing Him, and while you see Him not yet truly He sees you. He said: Then tell me about the Hour.[84] He said: The one questioned about it knows no better than the questioner. He said: Then tell me about its signs. He said: That the slave-girl will give birth to her mistress[85] and that you will see the barefooted, naked, destitute herdsmen competing in constructing lofty buildings. Then he took himself off and I stayed for a time. Then he said: O 'Umar, do you know who the questioner was? I said: Allāh and His Messenger know best. He said: It was Gabriel, who came to you to teach you your religion.[86]

Morality

Moral is that which is concerned with the principles of right and wrong conduct and morality is the quality of conforming to the principles of good conduct. The question which remains is: "How do we define right and wrong or good conduct?" Right and wrong may vary according to the perspective from which one views an action.

---

[83] In this context the word *iḥsān* has a special religious significance and any single rendering of it would be inadequate. Dictionary meanings for iḥsān include "right action", "goodness", "charity", "sincerity", and the like. The root also means "to master or be proficient at".

[84] i.e. of the Day of Judgement.

[85] This phrase is capable of more than one interpretation. Among those given by al-Nawawī in his commentary is that slave-girls will give birth to sons and daughters who will become free and so be the masters of those who bore them. The word amah, normally translated "slave-girl", is also capable of meaning any woman in that we are all slaves or servants of God. The words are thus capable of bearing the meaning: "When a woman will give birth to her master" i.e. a time will come when children will have so little respect for their mothers that they will treat them like servants.

The commentators point out that here the word *rabbah* (mistress) includes the masculine *rabb* (master).

[86] *Ṣaḥīḥ Muslim*, vol. 1, pp. 1-3, no. 1.

Standards of Morality

1. Philosophy:

Under capitalism, the unrestricted use of private property is considered morally good while under communism private ownership is morally evil.

2. Culture:

Inherited practices considered acceptable in one culture may be considered totally unacceptable in another. For example, when a national dance troupe from Papua New Guinea were invited to give performances in a variety of locations in Australia, the principle of a high school to which they were invited objected. He was attacked in the press for being narrow-minded, however, he refused to compromise and allow the bare breasted dancers to perform at his school.

3. Social Need:

Population control is critical in China; consequently for a woman to be pregnant for a second time is considered morally wrong in China.

When America was involved in World War two, atomic testing was morally sound to protect the country. After the atomic powers decided to ban nuclear testing, those who attempted to do so, like China, India, and Pakistan were judged to be morally wrong.

4. Professional Requirements:

According to medical ethics, psychiatrists do not reveal information about their patients even if they turn out to be psychopathic serial killers and people's lives are at stake.

5. Religion:

For Catholics, marriage is morally wrong for priests and nuns and information given in confessional is kept in confidence no matter how many lives may be threatened.

Democratic Morality

In the democratic system, moral values are set according to the preference of the majority. Consequently, it is inherently unstable and incomplete.

Islamic Morality

The Islamic system of morality is a complete system that governs human relations with God, with other humans and with the environment. It is morally good to worship God and morally evil to worship His creation. Preservation of one's life is morally good, while suicide is morally evil. Taking an animal's life for food or for clothing is morally good while killing an animal for sport is considered morally evil.

Foundation of Islamic Morality

1. Good and evil are according to God's definition. Allāh alone knows the ultimate consequences of actions. Consequently, He alone can absolutely define right and wrong. Good and evil may also be defined according to God's pleasure; what pleases Him is good and right and what displeases Him is wrong and evil.

2. What God has defined as permissible (Halāl) and forbidden (Ḥarām) is due to real benefit and harm existing in it, whether we are able to perceive it or not. These definitions are absolutely not arbitrary.

Fundamentals of Islamic Morality

1. Knowledge

In order to act in a morally correct way one must have knowledge or be capable of understanding what is right and wrong. Prophet Muḥammad (ﷺ) said, "*The pen is raised for the book of the child until it reaches maturity, the insane until he or she becomes sane and from the sleeper until he or she awakens.*"[87] Consequently, children, the insane and those unconscious are not held to be responsible for their actions.

2. Rational Choice

Errors due to accident or one being criminally forced by others are not considered to be sins. Prophet Muḥammad (ﷺ) said: "*Responsibility has been removed from my nation regarding acts done accidentally, out of ignorance or being forced.*"[88]

3. Proper Intent

Prophet Muḥammad (ﷺ) said,

> "*Deeds are judged by their intentions and everyone will be rewarded according to their intent.*"[89]

4. Taqwā

Prophet Muḥammad (ﷺ) said: *Iḥsān* is to worship Allāh as if you see him and though you cannot see Him you do so knowing that He sees you.

Great stress has been placed in Islām on good moral character. Prophet Muḥammad (ﷺ) summarized the essence of the Islamic message saying,

إنما بعثت لأتمم مكارم الأخلاق

"*Indeed, I was only sent to complete the most noble of character traits.*"[90]

---

[87] Collected by Abū Dāwūd, al-Nasā'i and Ibn Mājah, see *Sunan Abū Dāwūd*, no. 3822.

[88] *Sunan Ibn Mājah*, no. 2035.

[89] *Ṣaḥīḥ Al Bukhāri*, no. 1.

[90] Narrated by Abū Hurayrah and collected by al-Bukhārī in *al-Adab al-Mufrad*, al-Ḥākim and al-Bayhaqi in *Shu'ab al-Īmān*. It has been authenticated in *Ṣaḥīḥ al-Jāmi' al-Ṣaghīr*, vol. 1, p. 464, no. 2349.

And Allāh said in the Qur'ān:

وَإِنَّكَ لَعَلَىٰ خُلُقٍ عَظِيمٍ ﴿٤﴾

"Surely you (Muḥammad) have a magnificent character." Sūrah *al-Qalam* (68):4.

The Prophet's companion, Ibn 'Abbās explained that "character" here meant "religion", i.e., Islām.[91] By using the term "character" to refer to the religion of Islām, Allāh stresses the importance of morality in relationship to the religion. It was also reported that when the Prophet's wife 'Ā'ishah (﵂) was asked about the Prophet's character, she replied, "His character was that of the Qur'ān."[92] That is, his manners were according to Allāh's instructions in the Qur'ān. Consequently, the development of good character depends on closely following the Qur'ān and the teachings of the Prophet (ﷺ). In this regard, Allāh also said in the Qur'ān:

لَّقَدْ كَانَ لَكُمْ فِي رَسُولِ ٱللَّهِ أُسْوَةٌ حَسَنَةٌ

"Indeed you have in the Messenger of Allāh a beautiful example (of conduct)..." Sūrah *al-Aḥzāb* (33):21.

Thus, the rites and rituals of Islām cannot be separated from good manners. The Prophet (ﷺ) was reported to have said, "*Righteousness is good character.*"[93] Islām teaches man how to lead a morally righteous life by pointing out the proper way to live. Any Muslim who displays bad manners such as swearing or lying is either a hypocrite pretending to be a Muslim or a very

[91] *Tafsīr al-Qur'ān al-'Aẓīm*, vol. 4, p. 429.

[92] *Ṣaḥīḥ Muslim*, vol. 1, pp. 358-360, no. 1623, *Sunan Abū Dāwūd*, vol. 1, pp. 351-2, no. 1337 and *Aḥmad*.

[93] *Ṣaḥīḥ Muslim*, vol. 4, pp. 1358-9, no. 6196.

weak Muslim. Faith is inseparable from action. Abū Hurayrah quoted the Prophet (ﷺ) as saying, "*The believer whose faith is most complete is he whose character is best.*"[94] Consequently, throughout the Qur'ān, whenever Allāh instructs humankind to believe, He always links faith with the command to do righteous deeds. The Prophet did the same, saying, for example, "*Whoever believes in Allāh and the Last Day should be good to his neighbor and ḳind to his guest.*"[95]

That being the case, there should be an underlying principle of morality at the base of all Islamic teachings. Islām covers all aspects of human existence; spiritual, social and economic. Consequently, there is in Islām, a network of moral principles governing all human relations with God, with other humans, as well as with the environment in which humans exist. For example, from an Islamic perspective, worshipping others besides God would be considered morally wrong and bad character, in the same way that lying to others or littering the environment would be considered morally objectionable. Therefore, it may be assumed that each of the pillars of Islām and *Īmān* were designed to develop a particular set of moral characteristics. Without understanding the moral and spiritual goals of the pillars, they remain empty rituals which cannot benefit anyone in the next life.

---

[94] *Ṣaḥīḥ Sunan al-Tirmidhī*, vol. 1, p. 340, no. 928.

[95] *Ṣaḥīḥ Muslim*, vol. 1, p. 32, no. 76.

The Pillars of Islām

I. The *Shahādatān* (The Two Declarations of Faith)

The first pillar of Islām: لا إله إلا الله محمد رسول الله *lā ilāha il-lal-lāh Muḥammadur rasūlul-lāh* literally means "There is no god but Allāh, and Muḥammad is a messenger of Allāh".

A. Although the first part of the declaration لا إله إلا الله *lā ilāha il-lal-lāh* literally means "There is no god but Allāh", there are in the world many other gods being worshipped besides Allāh. Each of the many world religions has its own god, but, according to Islamic teachings, they are all false gods. Not merely because they have different names, but because they do not represent the true characteristics of God. Consequently, the first part of the declaration of faith actually denies the existence of any other true God besides Allāh. At the same time, it confirms that the true God is only One God, Allāh. Thus, the first declaration of faith would more accurately be translated as "There is nothing worthy of worship besides Allāh."

From an Islamic perspective, this declaration represents the foundation for human salvation, if it is based on knowledge. The Prophet's companion 'Uthmān quoted him as saying, "*Whoever dies knowing that there is nothing worthy of worship besides Allāh, will enter paradise.*"[96] If one makes this declaration in order to get married, or to please one's superiors, etc., it will be of no benefit in the next life, though one may achieve one's desires in this life on the basis of it. Marriage based on such a false declaration is invalid in the sight of God. If a woman marries a non-Muslim knowing that he is only declaring his faith in order to marry her, she is committing fornication. On the other hand, if someone declares the faith, they should be accepted as a Muslim until their actions or statements prove otherwise. 'Usāmah ibn Zayd said, "The Messenger of Allāh sent us on a raiding party. We raided the *Ḥuraqāt* clan of the Juhaynah tribe in the morning. I caught hold of a man and he said, 'There is no god but Allāh,' but I killed him with a spear anyway. Later it occurred to me to talk with Allāh's Messenger about it. He asked me, '*Did you ḳill him even though he declared that there is no god but Allāh.*' I said, 'O Messenger of Allāh, he only made the declaration out of fear of my weapon.' He replied, '*Did you tear open his heart to find out whether it had believed it or not?*' and he went on repeating it to me until I wished I had newly embraced Islām that day."[97]

B. The second part of the declaration of faith محمد رسول الله *Muḥammadur rasūlul-lāh* literally means "Muḥammad is a messenger of Allāh".

1. Acceptance of this article of faith means the acceptance of Prophet Muḥammad as the only infallible guide in life. It means obeying his instructions, whether the reasons behind them are understood or not. This absolute obedience is only due to Prophet Muḥammad's commands because they were based on revelation and were not a product of his own personal

---

[96] *Ṣaḥīḥ Muslim*, vol. 1, p. 19, no. 39.

[97] *Ṣaḥīḥ Muslim*, vol. 1, p. 56, no. 176.

whims and fancies. God stated the following, in this regard: "He does not speak of himself, [whatever he says] is only revelation revealed [to him]."[98] Consequently, obedience to the Prophet is obedience to God, as Allāh stated in the Qur'ān, "Whoever obeys the messenger has obeyed Allāh."[99] Obedience due to those in authority is qualified. The Prophet was quoted as saying, "*No creature deserves obedience [if it involves] disobedience to the Creator.*"[100]

2. Acceptance of Muḥammad's prophethood also means believing that he was the last messenger of God to humankind. Allāh declared him as such in the Qur'ān, "Muḥammad is not the father of anyone among you, but he is the Messenger of Allāh and the seal of the prophets."[101] Furthermore, the Prophet himself said, "*My similitude and that of the prophets before me is like that of a person who built an imposing and beautiful house, except that one brick [was missing from] one of its corners. People would circle the building appreciating it, but saying, 'Why hasn't the brick been placed there?' I am that [missing] brick and I am the last of the prophets.*"[102]

---

[98] Sūrah *al-Najm*, (55):3-4.

[99] Sūrah *al-Nisā'* (4):80.

[100] Collected by Aḥmad and al-Ḥākim and authenticated in *Ṣaḥīḥ al-Jāmi' al-Ṣaghīr,* vol. 2, p. 1250, no. 7520. Another narration of similar wording (لا طاعة في معصية إنما الطاعة في المعروف) can also be found in *Ṣaḥīḥ Al Bukhāri,* vol. 9, p. 271, no. 363 and *Ṣaḥīḥ Muslim,* vol. 3, p. 1022, no. 4535.

[101] Sūrah *al-ʿAḥzāb*, (33):40.

[102] *Ṣaḥīḥ al Bukahri,* vol. 4, p. 483, no. 735 and *Ṣaḥīḥ Muslim,* vol. 4, p. 1235, no. 5675.

C. Open Declaration : The declaration should be made publicly, except under circumstances where a person's life is at stake. For example, the Negus (ruler) of Ethiopia, who sheltered the first group of Muslims migrants from Makkah and later accepted Islām, hid his conversion from the majority of his people.

This declaration is not to inform God Who is already aware of man's beliefs. Allāh neither benefits from the acceptance of belief by human beings nor is He harmed by their disbelief. Thus, the declaration is not for Allāh's benefit, but for human benefit. The converts inform the Muslim community that they have become members in order to avail themselves of community support. Since faith increases and decreases, and the satanic / evil forces usually converge on the believers during their times of low faith, if the new believers are unknown to the community, they will not be able to benefit from their help. Consequently, the Prophet had warned the believers to hold fast to the community of believers. And Allāh warned that those who deviate from the way of the community will end up in hell.

The *Shahādatān* in Cultural Islām

From a cultural Muslim standpoint, a copy of the declaration beautifully written in Arabic calligraphy and elaborately framed is a must to decorate the walls of the living room. Muslim children are traditionally taught to recite the declaration, popularly known as the *ḳalimah,* as soon as they are able to speak. Furthermore, it is repeated in every one of the five formal prayers that Muslims are required to pray daily. However, it has no effect on the lives of cultural Muslims, because most have fallen prey to the delusion that being born in a Muslim family and having a 'Muslim' name guarantees them paradise, regardless of what they do in this life. This is a false belief, because Prophet Muḥammad expressly told his companion, ʿUmar ibn al-Khaṭṭāb, to inform the people that only the true believers would enter paradise.[103]

---

[103] *Ṣaḥīḥ Muslim,* vol. 1, p. 65, no. 209.

The character which the *Shahādatān* builds is:

a) an open personality

Believers are not secretive. They avoid secret organizations because their effect in society is mostly evil. Allāh discouraged secret gatherings saying:

﴿ لَّا خَيْرَ فِي كَثِيرٍ مِّن نَّجْوَىٰهُمْ إِلَّا مَنْ أَمَرَ بِصَدَقَةٍ أَوْ مَعْرُوفٍ أَوْ إِصْلَٰحٍ بَيْنَ ٱلنَّاسِ ۚ وَمَن يَفْعَلْ ذَٰلِكَ ٱبْتِغَآءَ مَرْضَاتِ ٱللَّهِ فَسَوْفَ نُؤْتِيهِ أَجْرًا عَظِيمًا ﴿١١٤﴾

> "There is no good in most of their secret talks except those who gather to encourage charity, righteousness or conciliation between people. I will give a great reward to whom-so-ever does that, seeking Allāh's pleasure." Sūrah *al-Nisā'* (4):114.

Although most secret organizations, like the Freemasons, Rosicrucians, etc., openly do charitable acts in order to win the confidence of the population, they primarily work in the interest of their members, even at the expense of the rights of others. For example, if a freemason is involved in a court case and he gives the secret mason hand-signal to the judge, who also happens to be a freemason, the judge will try his utmost to rule in favour of his fellow freemason.

In order to further discourage secretiveness and its pitfalls, Prophet Muḥammad was reported by Ibn 'Umar as saying, "*When three are present, two should not speak privately to the exclusion of the third.*"[104]

b) an honest personality

The believers are honest in their dealings with people. They do not present a smiling face to others while despising them behind

[104] *Ṣaḥīḥ al Bukhāri,* vol. 8, p. 203, no. 303.

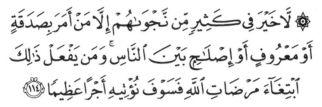

their backs. The Prophet said, "*The worst of people in Allāh's sight, on the Day of Resurrection, will be the two-faced person, who comes to one group of people with one face and to another group with a different.*"[105]

c) a missionary personality

If a person who accepts Islām truly believes that it is the only way of salvation for human beings, he or she would not hesitate to inform others about it. A Muslim could not possibly live and work along with non-Muslim neighbours and co-workers without informing them about Islām. In the Qur'ān, Allāh commands the believers to convey the message of Islām saying, "Call to the way of your Lord with wisdom and good speech."[106]

Prophet Muḥammad clarified that this responsibility is not restricted to specialists, scholars or missionaries. It is the duty of anyone who has some knowledge. He was reported by his companion, ʿAbdullāh ibn ʿAmr, to have said, "*Convey whatever you have learned from me, even if it is only a single verse from the Qur'ān.*"[107]

To hide such vital knowledge is considered a major sin in Islām. Allāh cursed those who hide religious knowledge in the following verse:

> "Verily those who conceal the clear proofs and guidance which I have revealed, after I made it clear for the people in the scripture, those are cursed by Allāh and cursed by all who would curse."[108]

---

[105] *Ṣaḥīḥ al Bukhāri,* vol. 8, p. 53, no. 84 and *Ṣaḥīḥ Muslim,* vol. 4, p. 1342, no. 6135 and p. 1374, no. 6300.

[106] Sūrah *al-Naḥl*, (16):125.

[107] *Ṣaḥīḥ al Bukhāri,* vol. 4, p. 442, no. 667.

[108] Sūrah *al-Baqarah*, (2):159.

The Prophet also said,

> *"Whoever hides knowledge will be branded with a branding iron from the hellfire."*[109]

II. *Ṣalāh* (Five Times Daily Prayer)

Formal prayer is instituted in Islām at five points of the day. It does not mean that a believer may not pray more than that if he or she wishes. It is natural for human beings to sometimes forget even the most important things. Humans often become so engrossed in fulfilling their material needs that they totally forget their spiritual needs. Five times daily formal prayer represents the bare minimum by which to organize the believer's day around the worship of God. The day of a human being tends to be structured around material needs. Waking in the morning to eat and prepare for work, breaking at lunchtime to feed, afternoon coffee breaks, breaking in the evening to eat and eventually to sleep. The body needs these breaks, however the soul also is in need of nourishment. Prayer is the primary source of nourishment for the soul.

The main purpose of prayer is the remembrance of God as stated in the Qur'ān:

إِنَّنِيٓ أَنَا ٱللَّهُ لَآ إِلَٰهَ إِلَّآ أَنَا۠

فَٱعۡبُدۡنِي وَأَقِمِ ٱلصَّلَوٰةَ لِذِكۡرِيٓ ١٤

> "Verily, I am Allāh, there is no god beside Me, so worship Me and establish regular prayer for My remembrance." Sūrah *Ṭā-Hā*, (20):14.

[109] Collected by Aḥmad, Abū Dāwūd, al-Nasā'ī and Ibn Mājah and authenticated in *Ṣaḥīḥ Jāmi' al-Ṣaghīr,* no. 6284, 6517.

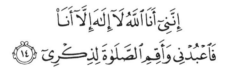

Remembrance of God is stressed because sin is generally committed when God is forgotten. The forces of evil operate most freely when consciousness of God is lost. Consequently, the satanic forces seek to occupy people's minds with irrelevant thoughts and desires to make them forget God. Once God is forgotten, people willingly join the corrupt elements. The final revelation, the Qur'ān, addresses this phenomenon in chapter *al-Mujādilah* as follows:

ٱسْتَحْوَذَ عَلَيْهِمُ ٱلشَّيْطَٰنُ فَأَنسَىٰهُمْ ذِكْرَ
ٱللَّهِ ۚ أُو۟لَٰٓئِكَ حِزْبُ ٱلشَّيْطَٰنِ ۚ أَلَآ إِنَّ حِزْبَ ٱلشَّيْطَٰنِ هُمُ ٱلْخَٰسِرُونَ ﴿١٩﴾

> "Satan has got the better of them and caused them to *forget Allāh*. Those are the party of Satan. Truly the party of Satan are the real losers." Sūrah *al-Mujadilah*, (58):19.

God, through Divine law, has prohibited intoxicants and gambling primarily because they cause human beings to forget God. The human mind and body easily becomes addicted to drugs and games of chance. Once addicted, humankind's desire to continually be stimulated by them leads them into all forms of corruption and violence amongst themselves. God says in chapter *al-Mā'idah* of the final revelation:

إِنَّمَا يُرِيدُ
ٱلشَّيْطَٰنُ أَن يُوقِعَ بَيْنَكُمُ ٱلْعَدَٰوَةَ وَٱلْبَغْضَآءَ فِى ٱلْخَمْرِ وَٱلْمَيْسِرِ
وَيَصُدَّكُمْ عَن ذِكْرِ ٱللَّهِ وَعَنِ ٱلصَّلَوٰةِ ۖ فَهَلْ أَنتُم مُّنتَهُونَ ﴿٩١﴾

> "Satan's plan is to incite enmity and hatred among you with intoxicants and gambling, and hinder you from the remembrance of Allāh and regular prayer. Will you not then abstain?" Sūrah *al-Mā'idah*, (5):91.

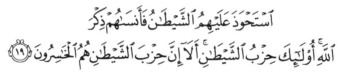

Consequently, humankind needs to remember God for their own salvation and growth. All humans have times of weakness in which they commit sins. If they have no means of remembering God, they sink deeper and deeper into corruption with every sin. However, those who follow the divine laws will be constantly reminded of God, which will give them a chance to repent and correct themselves.

Ṣalāh in Cultural Islām

Many cultural Muslims treat formal daily prayer quite casually. They consider the prayers merely as a means of accumulating good points on their record. Consequently, some only pray twice per year at the two annual celebrations (*ʿĪd al-Fiṭr* and *ʿĪd al-Aḍhā*), others only during the month of fasting, *Ramaḍān*, and yet others only pray the weekly Friday congregational prayer. Some regularly miss one or more of their daily prayers while others pray all five before going to bed at night. Yet others delay beginning regular prayers until their old age. The prayer is usually made very quickly without the least thought being given to what was said and done. The Prophet instructed those who prayed quickly to redo their prayers, because quick prayers are not counted.[110]

For cultural Muslims, the prayer has become such a ritual that in some parts of the Muslim world a special method of prayer was invented for women, distinct and different from the prayer of men. However, the Prophet instructed his followers to pray as he prayed, without making any distinction between males and females.

Consequently, non-Muslims will observe cultural Muslims praying regularly, yet being most dishonest and corrupt in their dealings with others. Yet, Allāh has stated in the Qur'ān that regular prayer prevents corruption,

---

[110] See *Ṣaḥīḥ al Bukhāri*, no. 751.

وَأَقِمِ ٱلصَّلَوٰةَۖ إِنَّ ٱلصَّلَوٰةَ تَنْهَىٰ عَنِ ٱلْفَحْشَآءِ وَٱلْمُنكَرِۗ

"Indeed formal prayer prevents evil speech and evil deeds." Sūrah *al-'Ankabūt*, (29):45.

Thus, if one's prayers do not prevent them from corruption, they are not performing the prayers which God has commanded.

The character which *Ṣalāh* builds is:

a) God-fearing

An individual who is conscious of God will question himself or herself prior to doing every act, "Is this act pleasing to God or not?" God-consciousness is the ultimate basis of righteousness, as it is that consciousness alone which will prevent an individual from evil, even when it is at his or her own expense.

b) Good speaking

True believers will not be noted for obscene language, slander, backbiting, lies, etc. During formal prayer, one is restricted to saying only good words as training for life beyond prayer. The Prophet (ﷺ) said, "*Let whoever believes in Allāh and the last day either speak good or be silent.*"[111]

c) Good acting

During formal prayer, the believer acts only in accordance with God's instructions. All of his or her body parts conform to set movements designed to train the believer to obey Allāh during the periods between the prayers. Consequently, what he or she looks at, hears, touches, walks to will be good. And the believer's interaction with people will be amicable. The Prophet (ﷺ) emphasized this concept saying,

[111] *Ṣaḥīḥ al Bukhāri*, no. 5671.

"*The religion is comprised of good social dealings.*"

III. *Zakāh* (Compulsory Charity)

The Arabs were known before Islām for their generosity. However, it was mainly for show. Islām recognised generosity as an admirable characteristic and made it an act of worship. The Prophet (ﷺ) was reported as saying, "*Whoever believes in Allāh and the Last Day should be generous to his guest.*"[112]

In all human societies the qualities of generosity and contentment are considered among the most noble characteristics. However, neither of these traits can develop if everyone has the same amount of wealth. Generosity can only be acquired when the human soul - aware that sharing with the needy is good - struggles against its desire to hoard its possessions. On the other hand, contentment is produced when the soul defeats the evils of envy and greed. The Creator wisely sets the stage for these spiritual struggles by unequally distributing wealth in this world. In chapter *al-Naḥl*, of the final revelation, Allāh says:

وَٱللَّهُ فَضَّلَ بَعۡضَكُمۡ عَلَىٰ بَعۡضٖ فِي ٱلرِّزۡقِۚ

"Allāh has favoured some of you over others in sustenance." Sūrah *al-Naḥl* (16):71.

Greed and stinginess are corrupt forms of the natural human desire to possess. The believers are informed by revelation that wealth is a trust given to humankind by God. Possessions exist in the world before humans are born and remain there after they die. If wealth is used according to divine instructions, it benefits those who have it in both worlds. But if it is used selfishly, it becomes a curse in this life and a cause for punishment in the next. In chapter

[112] *Ṣaḥīḥ al Bukhāri,* no. 5671.

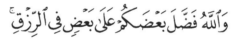

al-Anfāl of the final revelation, God warns the believers to beware of the dangers of wealth and children:

وَٱعْلَمُوٓا۟ أَنَّمَآ أَمْوَٰلُكُمْ وَأَوْلَٰدُكُمْ فِتْنَةٌ

"And know that your wealth and children are a test." Sūrah *al-Anfāl* (8):28.

God further warns the believers in chapter *al-Munāfiqūn* not to let their desire for wealth and children divert them from obedience to Him, for this is the test of possessions:

يَٰٓأَيُّهَا ٱلَّذِينَ ءَامَنُوا۟ لَا تُلْهِكُمْ
أَمْوَٰلُكُمْ وَلَآ أَوْلَٰدُكُمْ عَن ذِكْرِ ٱللَّهِ

"O believers! Do not allow your wealth and children to divert you from the remembrance of Allāh." Sūrah *al-Munāfiqūn* (63):9.

وَرَفَعَ بَعْضَكُمْ فَوْقَ بَعْضٍ دَرَجَٰتٍ لِّيَبْلُوَكُمْ فِى مَآ ءَاتَىٰكُمْ

"He raised some of you over others in rank to test you with what He granted you." Sūrah *al-An'ām* (6:)165.

The desire to accumulate wealth cannot be satisfied in this life. The more human beings have, the more they want. The Prophet (ﷺ) stated that,

> "*If a man had a valley of gold, he would desire another, for nothing will fill his mouth but the dirt [of his grave]. And Allāh forgives whoever sincerely repents.*"[113]

This negative desire can only be overcome by giving of one's wealth charitably. Thus, Allāh commanded the prophets to collect charity

[113] *Ṣaḥīḥ al-Bukhāri,* vol. 8, pp. 297-8, no. 447.

from the more wealthy among their followers for distribution among the poor:

خُذۡ مِنۡ أَمۡوَٰلِهِمۡ صَدَقَةٗ تُطَهِّرُهُمۡ وَتُزَكِّيهِم بِهَا

"Take charity from their wealth to purify them and make them grow." Sūrah *al-Tawba* (9):103.

Charity was institutionalized in Islām under the Arabic name, *Zakāh*[114] (compulsory charity) from its inception. Every believer with surplus wealth is obliged to give a set portion of it to the needy annually as an act of worship. To withhold *Zakāh* is considered a major sin. Giving this charity helps the believers to realise that their wealth is not their own to do with as they please. It teaches them that they are only temporary custodians of this wealth who must give a portion of it to those who are destitute. Consequently, God describes true believers as those who recognise the right of the needy to a portion of their wealth:

وَفِيٓ أَمۡوَٰلِهِمۡ حَقّٞ لِّلسَّآئِلِ وَٱلۡمَحۡرُومِ ١٩

"And in their wealth the beggars and needy have a right." Sūrah *al-Dhariyāt* (51):19.

However, giving in charity should be done sincerely for the pleasure of God, and not for show or control of others. The reward for charity is completely lost, when it is done for worldly gains. Allāh addresses this reality in chapter *al-Baqarah* as follows:

يَٰٓأَيُّهَا ٱلَّذِينَ ءَامَنُواْ لَا تُبۡطِلُواْ
صَدَقَٰتِكُم بِٱلۡمَنِّ وَٱلۡأَذَىٰ كَٱلَّذِي يُنفِقُ مَالَهُۥ رِئَآءَ ٱلنَّاسِ

"O believers, do not destroy your acts of charity by reminders of your generosity and by injury." Sūrah *al-Baqarah* (2):264.

---

[114] Literally *Zakāh* means 'purification' and 'growth'.

Craving for wealth is further enhanced by envy. Consequently, God also instructed us not to desire what He has given others. God addresses this issue in chapter *al-Nisā'*, of the final revelation as follows:

وَلَا تَتَمَنَّوْا۟ مَا فَضَّلَ ٱللَّهُ بِهِۦ بَعْضَكُمْ عَلَىٰ بَعْضٍ ۚ

> "And do not wish for that which Allāh has favoured some of you over others." Sūrah *al-Nisā'* (4):32.

The Prophet (ﷺ) reiterated this divine piece of advice saying,

> "*Look to those less fortunate than you, and do not look to those above you; it is better for you, in order that you do not deny what Allāh has blessed you with.*"[115]

When human beings focus their attention on those who have more wealth than they do, envy begins to develop. They usually feel and express that God has been unfair to them. Ultimately, they may commit many sins to fulfil their desire for what others have. Instead, Islām advises them to consider those less fortunate than themselves. No matter how difficult circumstances may be, there are always others in more difficult situations. Consequently, reflecting on others less fortunate reminds human beings of the many bounties with which God has blessed them. It is in this spiritual struggle of avoiding envy that the higher quality of contentment develops. Furthermore, according to the teachings of the prophets, material possessions do not constitute the real wealth of this world. Abū Hurayrah quoted the last Messenger (ﷺ) as saying,

> "*Wealth is not [measured] in property, but in contentment.*"[116]

---

[115] *Ṣaḥīḥ Al-Bukhāri,* vol. 8, p. 328, no. 497 and *Ṣaḥīḥ Muslim,* vol. 4, p. 1530, no. 7070.

[116] *Ṣaḥīḥ Al-Bukhāri,* vol. 8, p. 304, no. 453.

Being content does not mean that human beings should accept whatever circumstance they find themselves in and not try to better themselves. It means that, after striving to do one's best to achieve a good standard of living, one should accept what Allāh destines with a clear conscience. It is only by leaving one's affairs in the hands of God after making an effort, that the hearts find rest from the desires for the pleasures of this world. In this regard, God states in chapter *al-Raʿd* of the final revelation:

أَلَا بِذِكْرِ ٱللَّهِ تَطْمَئِنُّ ٱلْقُلُوبُ

"Indeed, it is in the remembrance of Allāh that hearts find rest." Sūrah *al-Raʿd* (13):28.

Zaḳāh in Cultural Islām

Among Muslims who do not understand the goals of *Zaḳāh*; it is common to find them neglecting this obligation. In fact, if all eligible Muslims paid their *Zaḳāh* regularly, the Muslim populations would be in a much better standing internationally than they are today. Most of the cases of UN relief agencies can be found in Muslim lands today, which should not be the case at all. Other cultural Muslims who go through the ritual of giving *Zaḳāh*, do so by giving to their needy relatives. Although this is technically permissible, it should not be the first option. Muslims are obliged to take care of their relatives at all times. If their relatives remain the most needy when the time of *Zaḳāh* distribution comes, it may also be given to them. Otherwise, it should be given to other needy members of the community, and voluntary charity should be given throughout the year to needy relatives.

The character which *Zaḳāh* builds is :

a) Generous

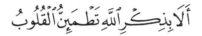

The believers are trained in generosity through *Zaḳāh*. Though it is only compulsory once every year, it was meant to develop a sense of generosity that would go beyond the obligatory to the voluntary. Consequently, the spirit of *Zakāh* should continue throughout the year and not be limited to one annual occasion.

b) Compassionate

Caring for others is universally recognised as one of the higher qualities that a human being may attain. *Zakāh* encourages the believers to reflect on the state of others. By seeking out the needy and helping them, a sense of compassion is developed in those who give the compulsory charity.

IV. *Ṣawm* (Fasting)

The Merits of *Ramaḍān*

a) The Prophet (ﷺ) was reported to have said that, "*When Ramaḍān comes, the gates of Paradise are open*."[117] The month of Ramaḍān is a great opportunity for one to do the deeds that could bring him or her closer to Paradise.

b) Fasting in Ramaḍān is also an opportunity to atone for one's sins. Abū Hurayrah quoted the Prophet (ﷺ) as saying, "*Whoever fasts during the month of Ramaḍān out of sincere faith and hoping for a reward from Allāh will have all of his previous sins forgiven*."[118]

c) Fasting also provides protection from evil for those who sincerely fast. Allāh's Messenger (ﷺ) was reported to have said, "*Fasting is a shield*."[119]

d) Allāh has a special reward which He personally gives to one who fasts faithfully. Abū Hurayrah related that the Prophet (ﷺ) quoted Allāh as saying, "*Every act of Ādam's descendants is for*

---

[117] *Ṣaḥīḥ al-Bukhāri*, vol. 3, p. 68, no. 122 and *Ṣaḥīḥ Muslim,* vol. 2, p. 524, no. 2361.

[118] *Ṣaḥīḥ al-Bukhāri*, vol. 3, pp. 69-70, no. 125.

[119] *Ṣaḥīḥ Muslim*, vol. 2, p. 554, no. 2565.

themselves, except fasting. It is meant for Me alone, and I alone will give the reward for it."[120]

e) Perhaps the greatest and most unique merit of Ramaḍān lies in the fact that the Qur'ān, which is the last and only unchanged book of Divine Guidance remaining in the world, was revealed during this month. Allāh states in Sūrah al-Baqarah..verse 185

شَهْرُ رَمَضَانَ ٱلَّذِىٓ أُنزِلَ فِيهِ ٱلْقُرْءَانُ هُدًى لِّلنَّاسِ وَبَيِّنَٰتٍ مِّنَ ٱلْهُدَىٰ وَٱلْفُرْقَانِ

> "The month of *Ramaḍān* is the one in which the Qur'ān was sent down as a (pure source of) guidance for mankind. In it are clear teachings showing the Right Way and the Criterion (for judging truth and falsehood)." Sūrah *al-Baqarah* (2): 185.

This act of revelation represents the greatest blessing from Almighty Allāh to mankind who had become steeped in darkness and ignorance since the time of the prior revelation. Without this supreme act of mercy, the weakening glimmer of guidance would have gone out completely and oppression would have reigned in all corners of the globe.

The Purpose of Fasting

The ultimate goal of the fast is to develop *Taqwā* (consciousness of God) in humans, as Allāh said in *Sūrah al-Baqarah* (2), verse 183:

لَعَلَّكُمْ تَتَّقُونَ

"...so that it may produce *Taqwā* in you."

---

[120] *Ṣaḥīḥ Muslim*, vol. 2, p. 559, no. 2566.

Taqwā is among the highest moral qualities that a Muslim can attain. It is produced by placing a shield between one's self and Allāh's wrath as the root meaning of the word implies (i.e. *Taqwā* comes from the verb *waqā,* which means "to defend"). This is achieved by being conscious of Allāh and all His commandments at all times, which means avoiding the *Ḥarām* (prohibited) as well as the *Makrūh* (undesirable) and even some of the *Halāl* (permissible) wherever doubt arises.

It has also been noted by medical experts that fasting improves the physical health in numerous ways. For example, during the fast the body uses up stored cholesterol (fats) which are often deposited in the blood system, as well as in other fatty areas of the body. Thus, it helps to keep the body firm and minimizes the danger of heart attacks.

Fasting in Cultural Islām

Where fasting has become a ritual, the month of *Ramaḍān* becomes a time of celebration instead of religious contemplation and abstinence. *Ramaḍān* nights are nights of party and enjoyment which continue until the dawn in some countries. There, the night becomes the day and the day becomes the night. In most places, the light meal which is supposed to be taken prior the dawn becomes a major three-course meal. Consequently, few experience real hunger during the fast. And at the time of breaking the fast, another three-course meal is taken, followed by a sampling of all kinds of sweets imaginable. As a result, many Muslims complain about gaining weight during *Ramaḍān*.

The character which *Ṣawm* builds is :

a) controlled

Since fasting is basically abstinence from food, drink and sexual relations, it trains the believers in self-control. Consequently, the actual test of the effects of fasting occurs at the time of breaking the fast. When food is traditionally spread out in large delicious quantities and people are tempted to gorge themselves, the believer is required to control his or her appetite and have a light meal and drink prior to the sunset prayers. It was the practice of the Prophet (ﷺ) to break his fast with three dates and water, and after the praying of sunset prayers eating a a moderate meal.

Fasting also means spiritual abstinence. It is required that the individual give up not only food, drink and sexual relations, but that he or she also restrain from all forms of lying, backbiting, slander, etc. This is confirmed by the Prophet's (ﷺ) statement, *"Allāh has no need for the hunger and the thirst of the person who does not restrain from telling lies and acting on them even while observing the fast."*[121]

He also said, *"When one of you is fasting, he should abstain from indecent acts and unnecessary talk, and if someone begins an obscene conversation or tries to pick an argument, he should simply tell him, "I am fasting."*[122] So, if one observes the fast according to the above principles, it should improve his moral character, making him more truthful and more careful about what he says and does.

b) moderate

Because the believer is required to restrain himself or herself at the time of breaking the fast, a sense of moderation in eating is developed. This is in keeping with the general recommendations given by the Prophet (ﷺ) regarding eating. Ibn ʿUmar, Abū Hurayrah and Abū Mūsā all quoted Allāh's Messenger (ﷺ) as saying, "*The believer eats in one stomach*[123] *and the disbeliever*

---

[121] Reported by Abū Hurayrah and collected by al-Bukhārī (*Ṣaḥīḥ al-Bukhāri* (Arabic-English), vol. 3, pp. 70-1, no. 127) and Abū Dāwūd (*Sunan Abū Dāwūd* (English Trans.), vol. 2, p. 648, no. 2355).

[122] Reported by Abū Hurayrah and collected by al-Bukhārī (*Ṣaḥīḥ al-Bukhāri* (Arabic-English), vol. 3, p. 71, 128), Muslim (*Ṣaḥīḥ Muslim* (English Trans.), vol. 2, p. 558, no. 2563) and Abū Dāwūd (*Sunan Abū Dāwūd* (English Trans.), vol. 2, p. 648, no. 2356).

[123] The Arabic term used is *miʿan* which literally means "intestine."

eats [as if] in seven."[124] Jābir reported that the Prophet (ﷺ) said, "*Food for one person is sufficient for two, and food for two can suffice four*."[125] Ibn ʿUmar related that the Messenger of Allāh (ﷺ) forbade anyone from taking two dates at a time without the consent of his eating companions.[126]

c) compassionate

Fasting gives the individual a real taste of hunger and thirst, which helps him to realise the experience of the poor. This experience should instill a desire to want to help those who are less fortunate by sharing food and wealth with them. This quality is emphasized by the ʿ*Īd al-Fiṭr* festival of fast breaking in which all Muslims are obliged to give the needy food to celebrate on that day.

V. *Ḥajj* (The Pilgrimage)

People of the world are usually aware of two kinds of journeys: journeys made to earn livelihood and journeys undertaken for pleasure and sightseeing. In both these types of journeys, people are impelled to go abroad by their material needs or their physical desires. They leave home for personal reasons and they spend their money or time to fulfil personal needs or desires. Therefore, no question of selfless sacrifice arises in such journeys, all sacrifices of wealth and time are for particular material returns, which are sought or expected. However, the journey which is called *Ḥajj*, is quite different from those other journeys. This journey is not meant to gain any personal end or to fulfil any desire. It is intended solely for Allāh; fulfilment of a duty prescribed by Allāh. No person can prepare himself to undertake this journey unless

---

[124] *Ṣaḥīḥ Muslim*, vol. 3, p. 1137, no. 5113.

[125] *Ṣaḥīḥ Muslim*, vol. 3, p. 1136, no. 5111.

[126] *Ṣaḥīḥ Muslim*, vol. 3, p. 1128, no. 5077.

he has true love of Allāh in his heart as well as fear of Him and feels strongly that this religious rite ordained by Allāh is obligatory on him. Therefore, whosoever sets out for *Ḥajj* leaving his family, his relatives, and his business, spending his money and patiently bearing the rigours of the travel, furnishes clear proof of his fear and love of Allāh. He proves that he possesses the strength to leave his home, face hardships, and willingly sacrifice his wealth and comfort when called upon to do so for the pleasure of Allāh.

The outward forms of worship in Islām fall under two general categories: physical, like *Ṣalāh* and *Ṣawm* and monetary like *Zakāh* and charity. *Ḥajj* combines both of these categories in its rites. It also simultaneously develops in man all of the spiritual and moral goals for the various forms of worship in Islām such as sincerity and piety, humility and obedience, sacrifice and submission etc. The physical demands of *Ḥajj* which involve circling the *Ka'bah*, walking between mounts Ṣafā and Marwah along with millions of others as well as journeying to Mina, Arafāt and Muzdalifah, far surpass those of *Ṣalāh* and *Ṣawm*. Thus, the self-control, humility and obedience produced by *Ṣalāh* and *Ṣawm* can all be found in pilgrimage to Makkah. Giving charity and *Zakāh* cleanses the heart of greed deposited by the love of this world. It builds generosity and develops in the individual a willingness to sacrifice for the sake of Allāh. *Ḥajj* serves a similar spiritual purpose as *Zakāh*; the pilgrim spends from his wealth and offers sacrifices in gratitude to Allāh and in order to win Allāh's approval.

During *Ḥajj*, one enjoys the privilege of offering many of his prayers in the great *Masjid* towards which he had been turning his face in prayer from his home along with the rest of the Muslim world. His prayers there are far superior in reward to similar prayers made anywhere else in the world. In fact, the Prophet (ﷺ) stated that a single prayer in *Al-Masjid Al-Ḥarām* in Makkah is worth one hundred thousand (100,000) prayers performed elsewhere.[127]

---

[127] *Mishkāt Al Maṣābiḥ*, vol. 1, p. 140.

However, there remain some even greater merits of *Ḥajj*. Two of which all true believers yearn for: self purification of sins and a guaranteed place in Paradise. The first of these two benefits was expressed by the Prophet (ﷺ) in the following simile, *"The person who makes pilgrimage to Allāh's house without committing any acts of indecency or disobedience to Allāh will return home as (pure from sins as) he was on the day his mother bore him."*[128] As for the second benefit, the Prophet (ﷺ) categorically stated: "*The reward for a Ḥajj Mabrūr (accepted into Allāh's grace) is nothing less than Paradise.*"[129]

The attainment of these benefits, as one can imagine, is not easy. Consequently, the routine performance of the rituals and rites of *Ḥajj* will not in itself earn these benefits. For *Ḥajj* to be accepted, it has to have an internal dynamism born of true and pure belief in God. It is this belief which drives the pilgrim to such spiritual heights that he or she is always consciously seeking the spiritual goals behind the physical rites and rituals of *Ḥajj*. It is only in this way that a pilgrim to the House of Allāh can avoid negative actions and reactions which may spoil his or her *Ḥajj*. During *Ḥajj*, one is thrown into the world's largest melting pot with little or no time to adjust. Conflicting habits and customs amidst the crush of the crowds are bound to cause misunderstandings. And, coupled with the fact that some pilgrims come to *Ḥajj* with dishonourable intentions, there is no way to avoid hurt feelings, bruised bodies and picked pockets (literally and figuratively). But just as it is only in the heat of the blast furnace that gold ore is separated from its impurities; likewise, it is only in the crush of bodies, customs

---

[128] Collected by *Ṣaḥīḥ Muslim*, *Ṣaḥīḥ Al-Bukhāri*, vol. 2, pp. 347-8, no. 596, *Mishkāt Al Maṣābiḥ*, vol. 1, p. 53 and *Riyāḍ-al-Ṣalihīn*, vol. 2, p. 615, no. 1274.

[129] *Mishkāt Al Maṣābiḥ*, vol. 1, p. 535, *Riyāḍ-al-Ṣālihīn*, vol. 2, p. 615, no. 1275, *Al-Muwattā' Imam Mālik*, p. 158, no. 756 and *Ṣaḥīḥ Al-Bukhāri*, vol. 3, p. 1, no. 1.

and emotions during *Ḥajj* that the striving soul of the pilgrim is purified and elevated. One cannot hope to attain the spiritual heights of *Ḥajj Mabrūr* by seclusion and the avoidance of crowds, because *Ḥajj* is contact with Allāh through contact with mankind. The Prophet Muḥammad (ﷺ) clearly pointed out the superiority of social interaction over isolation as follows: *"The believer who mixes with the masses and patiently bears their insults and offences is better than the one who neither mixes with the masses nor patiently bears their offences."*[130]

The *Ḥajj* which is graced by Allāh's acceptance has a lasting effect on the pilgrim. A deep spiritual transformation has taken place within the individual which can be observed in the over-all reconstruction of his or her life. The God-consciousness achieved during *Ḥajj Mabrūr* will cause the pilgrim to reform and call others to the most powerful tool of social, economic and spiritual reformation, namely Islām, in theory and in practice. If such a change does not take place and the pilgrim returns to the same un-Islamic life-style that he or she left behind; there can be not doubt that the *Ḥajj* of such a pilgrim was not graced by Allāh's acceptance. Such a *Ḥajj* merely removed the obligation of *Ḥajj* without earning for the pilgrim the higher spiritual rewards for which *Ḥajj* was designed and ordained.

Ḥajj in Cultural Islām

Ḥajj becomes legally obligatory when one reaches puberty and maturity. The commonly held belief in Muslim culture that it is better to delay *Ḥajj* until one becomes old is incorrect. It is based on a misinterpretation of a statement of the Prophet in which he said, *"Whoever makes a pilgrimage acceptable to Allāh, will return*

[130] *Mishkāt Al Maṣābiḥ*, vol. II, Book XXIV General Behaviour Chapter, II, p. 1055, *Ṣaḥīḥ Ibn Mājah*, vol. 2, p. 373, no. 3257.

home free from sin like the day his mother gave birth to him."[131] Cultural Muslims reason that one should delay *Ḥajj* until one becomes too old to do any more sins. In that way, *Ḥajj* would then wash away all of one's sins. However, the deliberate delay of *Ḥajj* is itself a sin, and one who chooses to continue in a life of sin is not likely to be able to make a pilgrimage acceptable to Allāh. The delayed *Ḥajj* is likely to be very ritualistic, and devoid of any spirit or sincerity. Consequently, when cultural Muslims return from the pilgrimage, they usually don certain outer garments (e.g. cap and scarf) to indicate to others that they made *Ḥajj* and they often adopt the title of "*Ḥajji*" with great pride. However, their inner lives have not changed in the least, indicating clearly that God did not accept their *Ḥajj*. For others, *Ḥajj* is an annual sight seeing tour. The "express" *Ḥajj* is designed for them in order to minimize the difficulty associated with the various rituals.

The character which *Ḥajj* builds is :

a) international / universalistic

The annual congregation of over two million Muslims from all corners of the globe representing all nations and tribes reminds Muslims that physical and biological differences are of no real consequence. All humans belong to one race, the human race. There is only One God Who created one race of human beings and ordained for them one religion. The pilgrimage also reminds Muslims that the political divisions in the world today which have resulted in the creation of nation-states, replete with their own national flags and anthems, should not supercede the Islamic Nation; the *Ummah*. The nationalistic feelings which drive those who watch cricket games to cheer for Pakistan or India, or those who love soccer to cheer Egyptian or Saudi teams, are antagonistic

---

[131] Collected by *Ṣaḥīḥ Muslim*, *Ṣaḥīḥ Al-Bukhāri*, vol. 2, pp. 347-8, no. 596, *Mishkāt Al Maṣābiḥ*, vol.1, p.53 and *Riyāḍ-al-Ṣāliḥīn*, vol. 2, p. 615, no. 1274.

to the *Ummah*-consciousness that Muslims are taught through the performance of *Ḥajj*. Though it is natural to love one's homeland, the land of one's birth, it should never lead to partisanship; where one defends one's family, tribe, nation even when they are in the wrong. Jundub quoted Allāh's Messenger (ﷺ) as saying,

> "One who is killed under a blind banner calling to tribalism or supporting tribalism, dies in a state of *jāhilīyah* (pre-Islamic ignorance)."[132]

b) patient

With so many people gathered together in particular locations performing the same religious rites, accidents are certain to occur. Toes will be stepped on and sides will be inadvertently bruised from the elbows of others. It is easy for a person to react violently under such circumstances. However, the pilgrim is obliged to patiently bear the harm of others in order to achieve an acceptable *Ḥajj*, whose reward is paradise, as promised by the Prophet.

---

[132] *Ṣaḥīḥ Muslim,* vol. 3, p. 1030, no. 4561.

The Pillars of *Īmān*

Faith in Islām is based on belief in six fundamental principles called the pillars of *Īmān*.

I. Belief in Allāh

1. Belief in Allāh begins with belief in His existence.

First and foremost, it should be noted that belief in God's existence is not illogical, as modern atheists would have mankind believe. Ancient Greek philosophers like Plato and Aristotle rationally concluded that God must exist. Plato argued from design that there must be a designer. When human beings come across footprints on a beach, they immediately conclude that a human being had walked there some time previously. It would be quite illogical to imagine that the waves from the sea settled in the sand and by chance produced a depression looking exactly like human footprints.

Consequently, it is not surprising to find that all human societies throughout human history, with very few exceptions, have believed in the existence of God. It is only in the 20th century that whole societies have been established based on the denial of God's existence. Russia and China and states under their control systematically taught atheism in all of their institutions of learning. However, after the fall of the soviet system and the abandonment of communist economics in China, the resurgence of religion in both countries has been phenomenal.

Anthropologists and psychologists have long held that belief in God was acquired by nurture. This was a natural result of their Darwinian views, which considered humans essentially animals, and thus the absence of religion among apes indicated that it must be man-made. In fact, Freud proposed that the oedipal-complex was the basis of human belief in God. Yet, some modern researchers increasingly leaned to the conclusion that belief in God must be natural for it to be so wide-spread. In 1997, experimental evidence for the inherent belief in God was found.

'God spot' is found in brain

by Steve Connor
Science Correspondent

SCIENTISTS believe they have discovered a "God module" in the brain which could be responsible for man's evolutionary instinct to believe in religion.

A study of epileptics who are known to have profoundly spiritual experiences has located a circuit of nerves in the front of the brain which appears to become electrically active when they think about God.

The scientists said that although the research and its conclusions are preliminary, initial results suggest that the phenomenon of religious belief is "hard-wired" into the brain.

Epileptic patients who suffer from seizures of the brain's frontal lobe said they frequently experience intense mystical episodes and often become obsessed with religious spirituality.

A team of neuroscientists from the University of California at San Diego said the most intriguing explanation is that the seizure causes an over-stimulation of the nerves in a part of the brain dubbed the "God module."

"There may be dedicated neural machinery in the temporal lobes concerned with religion. This may have evolved to impose order and stability on society," the team reported at a conference last week

The results indicate that whether a person believes in a religion or even in.

God may depend on how enhanced this part of the brain's electrical circuitry is, the scientists said.

Dr. Vilayanur Ramachandran, head of the research team, said the study involved comparing epileptic patients with normal people and a group who said they were intensely religious.

Electrical monitors on their skin—a standard test for activity—in the brain's temporal lobes—showed that the epileptics and the deeply religious displayed a similar response when shown words invoking spiritual belief.

Evolutionary scientists have suggested that belief in God, which is a common trait found in human societies around the world and throughout history, may be built into the brain's complex electrical circuitry as a Darwinian adaptation to encourage co-operation between individuals.

If the research is correct and a "God module" exists, then it might suggest that individuals who are atheists could have a differently configured neural circuit.

A spokesman for Richard Harries, the Bishop of Oxford, said whether there is a "God module" is a question for scientists, not theologians. "It would not be surprising if God had created us with a physical facility for belief," he said.[133]

---

[133] *The Sunday Times*, 2 Nov. 97, p. 1-9.

Consequently, of the many verses in the Qur'ān addressing God's attributes, only few address His existence.

In Sūrah *al-Ṭūr* (52):35-6, Allāh said:

أَمْ خُلِقُوا مِنْ غَيْرِ شَيْءٍ أَمْ هُمُ الْخَالِقُونَ ﴿٣٥﴾ أَمْ خَلَقُوا السَّمَاوَاتِ وَالْأَرْضَ بَل لَّا يُوقِنُونَ ﴿٣٦﴾

> "Were they created from nothing or did they create themselves. Or did they create the heavens and earth? Indeed, they are uncertain."

Logic and reason is used to convince humans that there must be a Creator. Allāh gives the three logical possibilities for human creation in these verses.

a) Humans were created from nothing or by nothing. This proposal violates basic reason. Something cannot come from nothing. Nothing cannot create something.

b) Humans created themselves. This is also an illogical and contradictory proposition. To create ones' self, one must already exist. But to be created one must first not exist.

c) Humans were created by something already created. This implies an infinite regression of causes which ultimately means that humans do not exist. If C1 were caused by C2, and C2 by C3 to CN, then C1 cannot exist unless C2 does, etc. And CN means that it has no beginning. Consequently, C1 cannot exist. In other words, if human existence is preceded by an infinite amount of causes requiring an infinite amount of time to take place, it is the same as saying that they will never take place. Human existence thus becomes impossible. The Greek philosopher Aristotle argued similarly that the infinite regression of the cause and effect chain was impossible.

The only remaining possibility is that humans and other created things were created by a being which is not itself created.

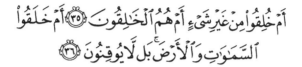

2. Belief in Allāh includes the belief that God alone is the Creator and Sustainer of this world.

Nothing takes place in the universe without His permission. No good can be obtained nor harm avoided unless Allāh decrees it. Humans are enjoined to seek refuge in the Lord of the Dawn from the evil of what He created.[134] Allāh does not attribute evil directly to Himself, because He is Good and all which comes from His is Good. The evil which comes from Allāh is relative evil. It may be good from other perspectives but evil in one perspective. For example, sunshine is essential for plants to grow and synthesize chlorophyll, yet it causes the rivers and lakes to dry up leading to drought, famine and death. Rain is also essential for plants to grow, yet it also causes floods, drowning and death. Pure evil, on the other hand, is a result of human activity. Humans think evil and, if Allāh permits it, they do evil. Allāh on the other hand does not oppress anyone:

وَلَا يَظْلِمُ رَبُّكَ أَحَدًا

"Your Lord does no wrong to anyone." Sūrah *al-Kahf* (18):49.

The evil which humans do is by Allāh's permission, so to that degree it is from Allāh. But humans are responsible for their evil because it is a product of their choice. Regarding God's permission, Muslim scholars of the past have distinguished between God's wish and His will. His wish is sometimes referred to as *His Legal Wish*, meaning that He wishes Islam for humans; the right way of life consisting of submission to whatever God has instructed. However, He also gave humans the ability to accept His wish or reject it. Consequently, humans may go against God's Legal Wish. His will, on the other hand, is referred to as *His Creational Will*, meaning that what takes place is by his permission alone. Among

[134] Sūrah *al-Falaq* (113):1-2.

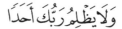

the things which take place are events beyond human will and events which are in accordance with human will. For example, humans are governed by the laws of "nature" which they cannot escape. If one jumps up, he or she must fall back down. If one's knee is struck by the doctor, the foot kicks out, no matter how hard the mind fights the reaction. Humans cannot go against Allāh's Creational Will.

When those who deny God's existence are asked why they are successful and others who have made similar or greater efforts are not, they reply that it is due to their good-fortune and the others' bad fortune. And when human life is analysed it is easily concluded that all of it is controlled by good and bad luck. Consequently, life is looked at as being controlled by the goddess of chance, *Tyche*, in Greek religion, and *Fortuna* in Roman. Religious rites involve, knocking on wood, crossing fingers, wearing amulets like four-leaf clovers, rabbits' feet, and horse shoes, while, at the same time, avoiding black cats, breaking mirrors, spilling salt, and the number 13. The goddess of fortune is more appealing to Western atheism because it is a blind force which does not require obedience nor assign obligations.

As a result of modern Western Civilisation's preoccupation with good luck, business men like Donald Trump, have been reported to fly over *Feng Shui* experts from Main-land China to guide their architects in the design of their buildings. And the commander of Apollo 13 responded to questions about any doubts he had concerning the lift-off by insisting that he should have known it was going to happen because the flight was Apollo number 13, which took off at 1300 hours (i.e. 1 o'clock) on Friday the 13th. Likewise, most high rise hotels, apartment buildings and office blocks do not have 13th floors, nor are houses numbered 13. Instead, floor 13 is renamed 14, and house 13 is labelled 12 ½.

Belief in Allāh requires the purification of the heart from any dependency on these and similar superstitions.

3. Belief in Allāh also means that God alone deserves human worship.

From an Islamic perspective, worship is not merely praising, honouring and offering sacrifices to a deity. To call on the deity for help is a fundamental part of worship. Consequently, calling on anyone other than Allāh in prayer is to worship them. The Prophet's companion, Nu'mān ibn Bashīr quoted him as saying, "[*Calling on anyone in*] *prayer is worship.*"[135] If one believes that nothing takes place except by God's will alone, it makes no sense to call on anyone other than God.

The character that belief in God builds is:

a) a God-conscious personality

As the five pillars of Islām all serve to develop God-consciousness through action and deeds, the first pillar of *Īmān* serves to provide a correct spiritual foundation to the desired state of God-consciousness. One who is aware of God knows that this life has meaning and purpose beyond the mere animal functions of eating, sleeping and sex.

b) a stable personality

By knowing that whatever happens is in accordance with God's will, gives the believer a sense of stability. The negative events of life are a part of a test and there is a good side to them which one may see, only if one is patient.

II. Belief in the Angels

Belief in the angels is fundamentally belief in their existence and in whatever has been revealed by God about their names,

---

[135] *Sunan Abū Dāwūd,* vol. 1, p. 387, no. 1474 and authenticated in *Ṣaḥīḥ Sunan Abī Dāwūd,* vol. 1.

attributes and roles. According to Islamic beliefs, there are three different species of created intelligent beings: mankind, angels and *jinn*. These intelligent beings are called *dhawul-'uqūl* (rational beings).[136] Although the bodies of human beings inhabit the visible material world, their souls inhabit the spirit-world of invisible rational beings. The spirit-world of created beings in the Islamic cosmological view is composed of human spirits, angels and *jinn*.

Angels, in Arabic *malak* (pl. *malā'ikah*), were created from light. According to the following statement of the Prophet (ﷺ) to his third wife, 'Ā'ishah (ﵐ), the daughter of Abū Bakr, *"The angels were created from light, the jinn from fire and Ādam from what has been already described to you."*[137] However, although the angels are made from light, it cannot be said that they appear as light, because they have not been described as such in either the Qur'ān or the authentic Sunnah. In their natural state, angels are invisible to human eyes. Angel Gabriel used to bring revelations to the Prophet (ﷺ) while he was in the company of his companions and none of them would see Gabriel. 'Ā'ishah (ﵐ) was quoted as saying, "Allāh's Messenger (ﷺ) [once] said to me, 'O 'Ā'ishah (ﵐ), here is Gabriel greeting you with peace.' I said, 'And may Allāh's peace and mercy be upon him. For he sees what I cannot.'"[138] However, angels are visible to some animals. The Prophet's companion, Abū Hurayrah reported that he said, *"If you hear a rooster crow, ask Allāh for His grace, for it has seen an angel."*[139]

---

[136] T.P. Hughes, *Dictionary of Islam*, p. 40.

[137] *Ṣaḥīḥ Muslim,* vol. 4, p. 1540, no. 7134.

[138] *Ṣaḥīḥ al-Bukhāri,* vol. 5, p. 75, no. 112 and *Ṣaḥīḥ Muslim,* vol. 4, p. 1302, no. 5997.

[139] Collected by Abū Dāwūd (*Sunan Abū Dāwūd,* vol. 3, p.1415, no. 5083), al-Bukhārī and *Muslim* (*Ṣaḥīḥ Muslim*, vol. 4, p. 1428, no. 6581).

In their normal state, angels are not human-like creatures with a pair of bird-like wings, as portrayed in Greco-Roman legends[140] and Christian influenced works of art.[141] Instead, they are normally huge in size and their wings may number anywhere from two to several hundreds. In this regard, Allāh said: "...making the angels messengers, with wings two and three and four; He increases in the creation as He wills..."[142] The companion, ʿAbdullāh ibn Masʿūd, reported that the Prophet (ﷺ) saw Angel Gabriel (Jibrīl) in his natural state in which he had six hundred wings, each of which filled the horizon. And there were multicoloured drops like pearls and coral falling from the wings.[143] In another narration, the Prophet (ﷺ) was reported to have said the following about Angel Gabriel, "*I saw him descending from the heavens and his great size filled the space between the earth and the sky.*"[144] Jābir ibn ʿAbdullāh quoted the Prophet (ﷺ) as saying, "*Allow me to speak about one of*

---

[140] Cupid, ancient Roman god of love, was the counterpart of the Greek god Eros. According to myth, Cupid was the son of Mercury, the winged messenger of the gods. He usually appeared as a winged infant carrying a bow and quiver of arrows. (*The New Encyclopaedia Britannica,* vol. 3, p. 796.)

[141] Cherubim (s. cherub) in Jewish and Christian literature are portrayed as celestial, winged beings with human and bird-like characteristics. (*The New Encyclopaedia Britannica*, vol. 3, p. 175.) In art, the four-winged cherubim are painted blue [symbolizing the sky] and the six-winged seraphim red [symbolizing fire]. (*The New Encyclopaedia Britannica,* vol. 10, p. 644).

[142] Sūrah *Fāṭir*, (35):1.

[143] Collected by Aḥmad. Ibn Kathīr rated its chain of narrators as *jayyid* (good). See *al-Bidāyah wa al-Nihāyah,* vol. 1, p. 47.

[144] Reported by ʿĀʾishah and collected by Muslim (*Ṣaḥīḥ Muslim*, vol. 1, pp. 111-112, no. 337).

the throne bearers.[145] *The distance between his ear lobe and shoulder is [what a bird would fly in]*[146] *seven hundred years.*"[147]

According to accounts from the Qur'ān and the *ḥadīth*, angels may take human form on certain occasions. An example from the Qur'ān may be found in the case of Mary, when Angel Gabriel came in human form to inform her of her impending pregnancy.[148] It is also recorded that Angel Gabriel used to visit the Prophet (ﷺ) in various human forms. Sometimes the Prophet's companions witnessed him visiting Prophet Muḥammad (ﷺ) in the likeness of a handsome companion by the name of Diḥyah ibn Khalīfah al-Kalbī,[149] and at other times in the likeness of an unknown bedouin.[150] However, in spite of the angels taking male human forms, they are not considered to be male or female,[151] nor is there any evidence in Islamic texts to indicate that they reproduce. In

---

[145] Qur'ān, (69):17, states that on the Day of Judgement Allāh's throne will be borne by eight angels.

[146] This explanation was given by Ibn Abī Ḥātim who collected the *ḥadīth*. See also an authentic narration of Anas ibn Mālik collected by al-Ṭabarānī in *al-Mu'jam al-Awsaṭ,* in which the distance is described as that flown by a bird.

[147] Collected by Abū Dāwūd (*Sunan Abū Dāwūd,* vol. 3, p. 1323, no. 4709) and authenticated by al-Albānī in *Silsilah al-Aḥādīth al-Ṣaḥīḥah,* vol. 1, p. 72, no. 151.

[148] Sūrah *Maryam*, (19):16-7.

[149] Collected by Aḥmad in *al-Musnad*, vol. 6, p. 146 and Ibn Sa'd in *al-Ṭabaqāt,* and authenticated in *Silsilah al-Aḥādīth al-Ṣaḥīḥah*, vol. 3, p. 105, no. 1111.

[150] *Ṣaḥīḥ al-Bukhārī,* vol. 1, p. 17, no.7 and *Ṣaḥīḥ Muslim,* vol. 1, pp. 9-10, no. 18.

[151] The stories of Hārūt and Mārūt yielding to sexual temptation, like those collected by Ibn Abī Shaybah, 'Abd ibn Ḥumayd, Ibn Abī al-Dunyā (in *Kitāb al-'Uqūbāt*), Ibn Jarīr, Ibn al-Munẓir, Ibn Abī Ḥātim and al-Bayhaqī (in *Shu'ab al-Īmān*), from the Jewish convert, Ka'b al-Aḥbār (see al-Suyūṭī's *al-Durr al-Manẓūr fī al-Tafsīr al-Ma'thūr*, vol. 1, pp. >

the Qur'ān the pagan Arabs are rebuked for referring to the angels as daughters of Allāh or even female.[152]

Although many names have been attributed to angels in Muslim folklore,[153] only a very few of their names have been verified according to authentic Islamic sources. Jibrīl (Gabriel) is the angel of revelation, Mīkā'īl (or Mīkāl, Eng. Michael)[154] is responsible for rain,[155] Isrāfīl[156] is the angel who will blow a horn (*ṣūr*) signaling the end of the world,[157] Mālik is the name of the main guardian angel of Hell,[158] Munkar and Nakīr[159] are two angels who will question each person following their death,

---

239-240), have led some Muslim theologians to conclude that angels have sex, but do not use it to propagate their kind. (See *Shorter Encyclopaedia of Islam*, p. 319). However, all of these narrations are inauthentic. The elements of these stories are found in a Jewish *midrash* as well as in the New Testament. (*Shorter Encyclopaedia of Islam,* p. 135).

152 Sūrah *al-Ṣāffāt*, (37):149-50 and *al-Zukhruf*, (43):19.

153 *Dictionary of Islam,* pp. 15-16.

154 See Qur'ān, (2):97-98.

155 *Sharḥ al-'Aqīdah al-Ṭaḥāwiyyah,* p. 336.

156 A loan-word with another dialectical variant "*Isrāfīn*" (*Mukhtār al-Ṣiḥāh,* p. 296), probably from the Hebrew word "Serafim" (*Shorter Encyclopaedia of Islam,* p. 184). It should be noted that descriptions of this angel, such as those found in the *Shorter Encyclopaedia of Islam,* p. 184, have no basis in authentic Islamic texts and are the product of legend and myths.

157 *Al-Bidāyah wal-Nihāyah,* vol. 1, p. 45.

158 Sūrah *al-Zukhruf*, (43):77.

159 Both names come from the Arabic root *nakira,* which means "to become bad, evil, abominable or foul." The word *munkar* literally means "any action deemed or declared foul, hateful or hideous" and *nakīr* means "disapproval, or the like, and manifestation thereof." (*Arabic-English Lexicon,* vol. 2, pp. 2849-2851).

and Hārūt[160] and Mārūt[161] were two angels sent to the people of Babylon as a test of their faith.[162]

The angels are in charge of the heavens and the earth. Thus, every movement which takes place in the world is a result of the [activities of the] angels.[163] Some angels are able to read human minds. The recording angels are aware of human intent and record the deeds that are intended but may or may not have been fulfilled. The Prophet (ﷺ) was quoted by his companion, Abū Hurayrah, as saying, "*The angels say [to Allāh], 'That man intends to do evil.' Although He is more vigilant than them. He replies, 'Watch him. If he commits evil, record it in ḳind; but if he abandons it, record for him one good deed. For surely he gave it up for My saḳe.*'"[164]

Angels are, by nature, obedient servants of Allāh and do not have the ability to disobey Allāh[165] and they are in constant contact with man. They play a variety of roles at all stages of human existence - from birth to death, and even beyond the grave.

They are assigned to the womb from the beginning of each human's conception until his birth, implementing Allāh's commands with respect to each individual. The Prophet's companion, Anas ibn Mālik, reported that he said, "*Allāh, the*

---

[160] Generally held to be a foreign name. (*Arabic-English Lexicon,* vol. 2, p. 2890).

[161] According to Arabic lexicophers, this word is either of foreign origin or it is derived from *murūtah,* which refers to the condition of a land which is desert without water or herbage. (*Arabic-English Lexicon,* vol. 2, p. 2703).

[162] Sūrah *al-Baqarah*, (2):102.

[163] *Sharḥ al-'Aqīdah al-Ṭaḥāwiyyah,* p. 335. See Sūrah *al-Nāzi'āt*, (79):5 and *al-Dhāriyāt*, (51):4.

[164] *Ṣaḥīḥ Muslim,* vol. 1, p. 75, no. 235.

[165] Sūrah *al-Naḥl*, (16):49-50.

Exalted and Glorious, has appointed an angel as the caretaker of the womb that says, 'My Lord, it is like an oily drop; my Lord, it is now like a leech; my Lord, it has become like a chewed clump.' Then, if Allāh wishes to complete its creation, the angel will ask, 'My Lord, will it be a male or a female?…'"[166] 'Abdullāh ibn Mas'ūd quoted the Messenger of Allāh (ﷺ) as saying, "*Each one of you is collected in his mother's womb for forty days, then becomes like a leech for a similar period. Then Allāh sends an angel and orders him to record four things: his livelihood, his life span, his deeds, and whether he will be wretched or happy. The angel then breathes the soul into him…*"[167] From his birth until his death, each person has been assigned an angel, inspiring him to do good and guarding him from evil. 'Abdullāh ibn Mas'ūd related that Allāh's Messenger (ﷺ) said, "Everyone of you has been assigned a companion from among the *jinn* and one from the angels…"[168] These angels are entrusted with the responsibility of guiding and advising each individual, by Allāh's will, to righteousness.[169] The Qur'ān also speaks about the guardian angels as follows: "For each [person] there are [angels] in succession[170] before and behind him. They guard him by Allāh's command…"[171] However, the guardian angels leave the humans

---

[166] *Ṣaḥīḥ al-Bukhāri,* vol. 8, no. 594, p. 388 and *Ṣaḥīḥ Muslim,* vol. 4, p. 1391, no. 6397.

[167] *Ṣaḥīḥ al-Bukhāri,* vol. 8, no. 593 and *Ṣaḥīḥ Muslim,* vol. 4, p. 1391, no. 6390.

[168] Collected by Aḥmad in *al-Musnad* and Muslim (referred to by number only in *Ṣaḥīḥ Muslim,* vol. 4, p. 1472, no. 6758). See *Ṣaḥīḥ Muslim, Sharḥ al-Nawawī,* vol. 17, p. 158 for the full Arabic text, the English of which has been deleted in the aforementioned translation.

[169] See *al-Bidāyah wal-Nihāyah,* vol. 1, p. 52.

[170] The Arabic term used in the verse is *mu'aqqibāt,* which Ibn 'Abbās interpreted to mean angels who would protect each person until something destined by Allāh is afflicted upon him. See *al-Bidāyah wal-Nihāyah,* vol. 1, p. 50.

[171] Sūrah *al-Ra'd*, (13):11.

to whom they are assigned on certain occasions. For example, Abū Ṭalḥah reported that Prophet Muḥammad (ﷺ) said, "*The angels do not enter a house in which there is a dog or pictures, or statues of living creatures.*"[172] Two angels are also assigned to every human being with the duty of recording their deeds. The Qur'ān refers to them in the following verses: "But verily, watching over you [are appointed angels], kind and honourable, writing down [your deeds]."[173] Abū Umāmah reported that Prophet Muḥammad (ﷺ) described them as follows, "*Surely, the [angel on the] left raises the pen [from the record] of a Muslim who commits an error for six hours. If he repents and asks Allāh's forgiveness, the deed is cast aside, otherwise it is written down as one [evil deed].*"[174]

According to Prophet Muḥammad (ﷺ), there are also angels that pray to Allāh on behalf of humans on specific occasions. For example, he was reported to have said, "*As long as any one of you is waiting for prayer, or he is in prayer, the angels [continue to] say, 'O Allāh, be merciful to him and forgive him,' as long as he does not leave his place of prayer or pass wind.*"[175]

Some angels have been assigned the job of extracting human souls from their bodies at the time of their death. Reference is made to these angels in the Qur'ān as follows: "He is the Irresistible, far above His servants. He sets guardians over you until death comes to one of you, then His angels take your soul without fail."[176] Yet others have been given the duty of taking the extracted soul on a spiritual journey out of this world and back into it. Al-Barā' ibn 'Āzib stated that the Prophet (ﷺ) said, "*When a believer is leaving*

---

[172] *Ṣaḥīḥ al-Bukhāri,* vol. 4, pp. 297-298, no. 448.

[173] Sūrah *al-Infiṭār*, (82):10-11. See also *Qāf*, (50):17-8.

[174] Collected by al-Ṭabarānī in *al-Mu'jam al-Kabīr* and authenticated (*ḥasan*) by al-Albānī in *Ṣaḥīḥ al-Jāmi' al-Ṣaghīr*, vol. 2, p. 422, no. 2097.

[175] *Ṣaḥīḥ al-Bukhāri,* vol. 4, p. 299, no. 452.

[176] Sūrah *al-Sajdah*, (32):11 and *al-An'ām*, (6):61.

this world and entering the next, angels with faces shining brightly like the sun descend from the heavens carrying a shroud and embalming fragrance from Paradise, and [then they] sit down within sight-range. The Angel of Death then approaches, sits by his head and says, 'O good soul, come out to Allāh's forgiveness and pleasure.' It will then come out like a flowing drop of water from a water-skin, and he will catch it. But, within the blinking of an eye after he catches it, they will take it and put it in the shroud and fragrance. There will then come from the soul a fragrance like that of the sweetest musk found on the face of the earth. They then ascend with it and every group of angels they pass ask, 'Who is this good soul?' to which they reply, 'So-and-so, the son of So-and-so,' using his best names by which people called him on earth. They then bring him to the lowest heaven and ask that the gate should be opened for him. This is done, and from every heaven its archangels escort him to the next heaven until he is brought to the seventh heaven, and Allāh, Most Great and Glorious, says, 'Record the book of My servant in the 'illiyyūn' [register of the righteous][177] *and take him back to earth, for I created mankind from it, and I shall return them to it, and from it I shall bring them forth again.'*[178] *His soul is then restored to his body…*"[179]

Another two angels, Munkar and Nakīr, are charged with questioning the soul in the grave. In a continuation of the previous *ḥadīth*, the Prophet (ﷺ) went on to say, "*Two angels come to him, make him sit up and ask him, 'Who is your Lord?' He [the believing*

---

177 "But, verily the record of the righteous is [preserved] in *'illiyyūn*. And what will explain to you what *'illiyyūn* is? It is a book of records." Qur'ān, 83, (18):20.

178 This statement coincides with the following Qur'ānic verse: "From it We created you, into it We will return you, and from it We will bring you forth again." Qur'ān, (20):55.

179 Collected by Aḥmad (*Mishkāh al-Maṣābīḥ*, vol. 1, pp. 340-342) and Abū Dāwūd (*Sunan Abū Dāwūd*, vol. 3, p. 1330, no. 4735) and authenticated by al-Albānī in *Ṣaḥīḥ al-Jāmi' al-Ṣaghīr*, vol. 1, pp. 344-346, no. 1676.

soul] will reply, 'My Lord is Allāh.' They will then ask, 'What is your religion?' and he will reply, 'My religion is Islām.' They will ask, 'Who is this man who was sent among you?' and he will say, 'He is the Messenger of Allāh.' They will then ask, 'What was the [sources of] your knowledge?' and he will reply, 'I have read Allāh's Book, believed in it and declared it to be true.'"[180]

The main characteristic that belief in the angels builds is:

A deliberate and careful personality

Angels are a part of the forces in God's creation which human science would never discover, no matter how advanced human technology reached. Whether humans believe in angels or consider them superstition, does not affect Allāh in any way. Allāh chose to inform human beings about the world of the angels for their own good. Humans are the ones who benefit from information about angels and their roles in human life. Knowledge that all of humankind's deeds and even their thoughts are being constantly recorded causes the intelligent among them to think before acting. The true believer avoids hasty actions based on the Prophet's recommendation, "*Careful and deliberate action is from Allāh, and haste is from satan.*"[181]

Belief in the *Jinn*

Belief in the world of the angels includes belief in the other creatures of the unseen 'spiritual' world, the *Jinn*. Although modern Muslims tend to brush off information about this world due to implausibility of popular myths and superstitions regarding them, Allāh spoke about them in the seventy-second chapter of the Qur'ān known as *al-Jinn*, as well as in a number of other chapters.

---

[180] See also *Ṣaḥīḥ al-Bukhāri*, vol. 2, pp. 257-258, no. 456.

[181] Collected by al-Tirmidhi.

The term *jinn* comes from the verb جَنَّ *jannah* which means "to cover, hide or conceal". They represent another creation of Allāh which co-exists with humans on the earth. Allāh created the *jinn* before He created the human race from a different set of elements than those used to create the first human. Allāh said, "Verily, I created man from dried clay, from black putrid mud. And I created the *jinn* before that from a fiery wind."[182] They were named *Jinn* because they are hidden from the eyes of mankind. Iblīs (Satan) is from the world of the *Jinn*.

The *Jinn* may first be divided into three broad categories in relation to their modes of existence. The Prophet (ﷺ) said: "*There are three types of Jinn: One type which flies in the air all the time, another type which exists as snakes and dogs, and an earthbound type which resides in one place or wanders about.*"[183]

The *Jinn* may be further divided into two categories in relationship to their faith: Muslims (believers) and *Kāfirs* (disbelievers).[184] The disbelievers among the *Jinn* are referred to by various names in both Arabic and English: *ʿIfrīt, Shayṭān, Qarīn,* demons, devils, spirits, ghosts, etc. They try to misguide man in various ways. Whoever listens to them and becomes a worker for them is referred to as a human devil. Allāh said: "Likewise, we have made for every Prophet an enemy, devils from among mankind and the *Jinn*."[185]

Every human has an individual *Jinn* accompanying him referred to as a *Qarīn* (i.e. companion). This is a part of man's test in this life. The *Jinn* encourage his lower desires and constantly try to divert him from righteousness. The Prophet (ﷺ) referred to

---

[182] Sūrah *al-Ḥijr*, (15):26-7.

[183] Collected by al-Ṭabarī and al-Ḥākim.

[184] Sūrah *al-Jinn*, (72):1-4 and 14-5.

[185] Sūrah *al-Anʿām*, (6):112.

this relationship as follows, "*Everyone of you has been assigned a companion from the Jinn.*" The companions asked, "*Even you, O Messenger of Allāh?*" And the Prophet replied, "*Even me, except that Allāh has helped me against him and he has submitted. Now he only tells me to do good.*"[186]

Prophet Sulaymān (Solomon) was given miraculous control over the *Jinn*, as a sign of his prophethood.[187] But this power was not given to anyone else. No one else is allowed to control the *Jinn* and no one can. The Prophet (ﷺ) said, "*Verily an ʿIfrīt*[188] *from among the Jinn spat on me last night trying to break my Ṣalāh. However Allāh let me overpower him and I wanted to tie him to one of the columns in the masjid so that you all could see him in the morning. Then, I remembered my brother Sulaymān's prayer:* 'O my Lord, forgive me and bestow on me a kingdom not allowed to anyone after me.'[189]"[190]

Fortune-telling

Human beings cannot gain control over the *Jinn* as this was a special miracle given only to Prophet Sulaymān. In fact, contact with the *Jinn* in circumstances other than possession, or accident is most often made by the performance of sacrilegious acts despised and forbidden in the religion.[191] The evil *Jinn* summoned in this fashion may aid their partners in sin and disbelief in God. Their

---

[186] *Ṣaḥīḥ Muslim*, vol. 4, p. 1472, no. 6757.

[187] Sūrah *al-Naml*, (27):17.

[188] A strong or powerful evil *Jinn* (E.W.Lane, Arabic-English Lexicon, (Cambridge, England: Islamic Texts Society, 1984), vol. 2, p. 2089.

[189] Sūrah *Ṣād* (38):35.

[190] *Ṣaḥīḥ al-Bukhāri*, vol. 1, p. 268, no. 75 and *Ṣaḥīḥ Muslim*, vol. 1, p.273, no. 1104.

[191] Abū Ameenah Bilal Philips, Ibn Taymiyyah's Essay on the *Jinn*, (Riyadh: Tawḥīd Publications, 1989), p. 21.

goal is to draw as many others as they can into the gravest of sins, the worship of others besides or along with God. Once contact and contract with the *Jinn* are made by fortune-tellers, the *Jinn* may inform them of certain events in the future. The Prophet (ﷺ) described how the *Jinn* gather information about the future. He related that the *Jinn* were able to travel to the lower reaches of the heavens and listen in on some of the information about the future, which the angels pass among themselves. They would then return to the earth and feed the information to their contacts.[192] This used to happen a lot prior to the prophethood of Muḥammad (ﷺ) and fortune-tellers were very accurate in their information. They were able to gain positions in the royal courts and enjoyed much popularity and were even worshipped in some religions of the world.

After the Prophet Muḥammad (ﷺ) began his mission, the situation changed. Allāh had the angels guard the lower reaches of the heavens carefully, and most of the *Jinn* were chased away with meteors and shooting stars.[193] The Prophet's companion, Ibn ʿAbbās, said, "When the Prophet (ﷺ) and a group of his companions set out for the Ukāẓ market, the devils were blocked from hearing information in the heavens. Meteors were let loose on them, so they returned to their people. When their people asked what happened, they told them. Some suggested that something must have happened, so they spread out over the earth seeking the cause. Some of them came across the Prophet and his companions while they were in prayer and they heard the Qur'ān. They said to themselves that this must have been what blocked them from listening. When they returned to their people they told them, 'Verily we have heard a marvellous Qur'ān. It guides unto righteousness so we believed in it. And we will never

---

[192] *Ṣaḥīḥ Muslim*, vol. 4, p. 1210, no. 5538.

[193] Sūrahs *al-Jinn* (72):8-9 and *al-Ḥijr* (15):17-18.

make partners with our Lord.'[194]"[195] Thus, the *Jinn* could no longer gather information about the future as easily as they could before the Prophet's (ﷺ) mission. Because of that, they now mix their information with many lies. The Prophet (ﷺ) said: "*They (the Jinn) would pass the information back down until it reaches the lips of a magician or fortune-teller. Sometimes a meteor would overtake them before they could pass it on. If they passed it on before being struck, they would add to it a hundred lies.*"[196] 'Ā'ishah (رضي الله عنها), third wife of the Prophet (ﷺ), reported that when she asked him about fortune-tellers, he replied that they were nothing. She then mentioned that the fortune-tellers sometimes told things which were true. The Prophet (ﷺ) said: "*That is a bit of truth which the Jinn steals and cackles in the ear of his friend; but he mixes along with it a hundred lies.*"[197]

The *Jinns* are also able to inform their human contact of the relative future. For example, when someone comes to a fortune-teller, the fourtuneteller's *Jinn* gets information from the man's *Qarīn*[198] of what plans he had made prior to his coming. So the fortune-teller is able to tell him that he will do this or that, or go here or there. By this method, the real fortune-teller is also able to learn about a stranger's past in vivid detail. He is able to tell a total stranger of his parents' names, where he was born, the acts of his childhood, etc. The ability to vividly describe the past is one of the marks of a true fortune-teller who has made contact with the *Jinn*. Because the *Jinn* are able to traverse huge

---

[194] Sūrah *al-Jinn* (72):1-2.

[195] *Ṣaḥīḥ al-Bukhāri*, vol. 6, pp. 415-16, no. 443, *Ṣaḥīḥ Muslim*, vol. 1, pp. 243-44, no. 908, *al-Tirmidhī* and *Aḥmad*.

[196] *Ṣaḥīḥ al-Bukhāri*, vol. 8, p. 150, no. 2320 and *al-Tirmidhī*.

[197] *Ṣaḥīḥ al-Bukhāri*, vol. 7, p. 439, no. 657 and *Ṣaḥīḥ Muslim*, vol. 4, p. 1209, no. 5535.

[198] The *Jinn* assigned to every human being.

distances instantaneously, they are also able to gather huge stores of information about hidden things, lost articles and unobserved events. Proof of this ability can be found in the Qur'ān, in the story about Prophet Sulaymān and Bilqīs, the Queen of Sheba. When Queen Bilqīs came to see him, he asked the *Jinn* to bring her throne from her land. "An ʿ*Ifrīt* from among the *Jinns* said, "I will bring it for you before you can get up from your place. Verily, I am strong and trustworthy for the assignment."[199]

Because of the sacrilege and heresy involved in fortune-telling, Islām has taken a very strong stance towards it. Islām opposes any form of association with those who practise fortune-telling, except to advise them to give up their forbidden practices. The Prophet (ﷺ) laid down principles which clearly forbade any form of visitation of fortune-tellers. Ṣafiyah reported from Ḥafṣah (wife of the Prophet (ﷺ)) that the Prophet (ﷺ) said, "*The Ṣalāh of whoever approaches a fortune-teller and asks him about anything will not be accepted for 40 days and nights.*"[200] The punishment in this tradition is for simply approaching a fortune-teller and asking him questions out of curiosity. This prohibition is further supported by Muʿāwiyah ibn al-Ḥakam al-Salamī's report in which he said, "O Messenger of Allāh, verily there are some people among us who visit oracles." The Prophet (ﷺ) replied, "*Do not go to them.*"[201] Such a severe punishment has been assigned for only visitation because it is the first step to belief in fortune-telling. If one went there doubtful about its reality, and some of the fortune-teller's predictions come true, one will surely become a true devotee of the fortune-teller and an ardent believer in fortune-telling.

The individual who approaches a fortune-teller is still obliged to make his compulsory prayers throughout the 40 day period,

---

[199] Sūrah *al-Naml* (27):39-40.

[200] *Ṣaḥīḥ Muslim*, vol. 4, p. 1211, no. 5540.

[201] Ibid., p. 1209, no. 5532.

even though he gets no reward from his prayers. If he abandons the prayer all together, he has committed an even greater sin. Whenever obligatory prayer is performed, it produces two results under normal circumstances: (1) It removes the obligation of that prayer from the individual, and (2) It earns him a reward. Consequently, though the reward is lost for 40 days, the obligation still remains.

The Islamic ruling with regard to anyone who visits a fortune-teller believing that he knows the unseen and the future is that of *Kufr* (disbelief). The Prophet's companions, Abū Hurayrah and al-Ḥasan both reported from the Prophet (ﷺ) that he said, "*Whosoever approaches a fortune-teller and believes what he says, has disbelieved in what was revealed to Muḥammad.*"[202] Belief in fortune-tellers assigns to creation some of Allāh's attributes with regard to knowledge of the unseen and the future. Consequently, it destroys faith in the Unique Oneness of Allāh (*tawḥīd*) and represents a form of *Shirk* (idolatry). The ruling of *Kufr* includes, by analogy (*Qiyās*), those who read the books and writings of fortune-tellers, listen to them on the radio, watch them on the T.V., or find them in computer programs, as these are the most common means used by 20th century fortune-tellers to spread their predictions. Therefore, all the various methods used around the world by oracles, fortune-tellers, and the likes, are forbidden to Muslims. Palm-reading, I-Ching, fortune cookies, tea leaves as well as Zodiacal signs and Bio-rhythm computer programs, all claim to inform those who believe in them about their future. However, Allāh has stated in no uncertain terms that He alone knows the future:

إِنَّ ٱللَّهَ عِندَهُۥ عِلْمُ ٱلسَّاعَةِ وَيُنَزِّلُ ٱلْغَيْثَ

---

[202] Collected by Aḥmad. Abū Dāwūd (*Sunan Abū Dāwūd* (English Trans.), vol. 3, p. 1095, no. 3895) and *al-Bayhaqī*.

وَيَعْلَمُ مَا فِي ٱلْأَرْحَامِ ۖ وَمَا تَدْرِى نَفْسٌ مَّاذَا تَكْسِبُ غَدًا ۖ
وَمَا تَدْرِى نَفْسٌۢ بِأَىِّ أَرْضٍ تَمُوتُ ۚ إِنَّ ٱللَّهَ عَلِيمٌ خَبِيرٌۢ ﴿٣٤﴾

"Verily the knowledge of the Hour is with Allāh alone. It is He who sends down the rain and knows the contents of the wombs. No one knows what he will earn tomorrow nor in which land he will die, but Allāh is all-knowing and aware."[203]

Therefore, Muslims must take utmost care in dealing with books, magazines, newspapers as well as individuals who, in one way or another, claim knowledge of the future or the unseen. For example, when a Muslim weather-man predicts rain, snow, or other climatic conditions for tomorrow he should add the phrase, "*Inshā Allāh* (If Allāh wishes)." Likewise, when the Muslim doctor informs her patient that she will deliver a child in 9 months or on such and such a day, she should take care to add the phrase *Inshā Allāh,* as such statements are only estimations based on statistical information.

Magic

The other major area in which the *jinn* interfere with the human world is the realm of magic. Although it has become popular in modern times to deny that magic has any reality to it all, magical shows continue to intrigue and entertain large audiences in the West. Popular Eastern stories about the effects of 'black' magic are explained away as the result of psychological disorders like hysteria, etc., and it is often pointed out that magic only affects those who believe in it.[204] Magical feats are all described as hoaxes based on a series of illusions and tricks.

---

[203] Sūrah *Luqmān*, (31):34.

[204] The Ash'arite scholar, Fakhrud-Dīn al-Rāzī (d.1210CE) proposed this idea in his commentary on verse 102 of Sūrah *al-Baqarah* and the noted historian, Ibn Khaldūn further developed it.

In spite of the fact that Islām rejects the effects of charms and amulets with regards to the prevention of misfortune and the attraction of good fortune, it does recognise that some aspects of magic are real. It is true that much of the magic around today is a product of trickery involving gadgets cleverly designed to deceive audiences. But, just as in the case of fortune-telling, there exist around the world some people who practise real magic resulting from their contact with the *Jinns*. Allāh, in the Qur'ān explains the fundamental Islamic view of magic in the following verse:

وَٱتَّبَعُوا۟ مَا تَتْلُوا۟ ٱلشَّيَٰطِينُ عَلَىٰ مُلْكِ سُلَيْمَٰنَ ۖ وَمَا كَفَرَ
سُلَيْمَٰنُ وَلَٰكِنَّ ٱلشَّيَٰطِينَ كَفَرُوا۟ يُعَلِّمُونَ ٱلنَّاسَ
ٱلسِّحْرَ

> "They (Jews) follow what the devils related concerning Solomon's kingdom, but it was not Solomon who disbelieved, it was the devils who disbelieved by teaching the people magic."[205]

The Jews used to justify their practice of magic within an esoteric mystical system called the *Cabala* by claiming that they had learned it from Prophet Sulaymān himself. The Jews who learned these arts knew well that they were cursed because it was forbidden in their own scriptures. The following verses can still be found in the Torah:

> "When you come into the land which the Lord your God gives you, you shall not learn to follow the abominable practices of those nations. There shall not be found among you anyone who burns his son or his daughter as an offering, anyone who practises divination, a soothsayer, or an auger, or a sorcerer, or a charmer, or a medium, or a wizard, or a necromancer. For whoever does these things is an abomination to the Lord; and

---

[205] Sūrah *al-Baqarah*, (2):102.

because of these abominable practices the Lord your God is driving them out before you."[206]

There are also authentic traditions which mention that on one occasion the Prophet (ﷺ) himself suffered from the effects of magic. The Prophet's companion, Zayd ibn Arqam reported that a Jew by the name of Labīb ibn A'ṣam, cast a magical spell on the Prophet (ﷺ) and when he began to suffer from it, Jibrīl came to him and revealed the *Mu'awwidhatān* (Sūrahs *al-Falaq* and *al-Nās*) then said to him, "Surely it was a Jew who cast this spell on you and the magical charm is in a certain well." The Prophet sent 'Alī ibn Abī Ṭālib to go and fetch the charm. When he returned with it, the Prophet (ﷺ) told him to unite the knots in it, one by one, and recite a verse from the Sūrahs with each. When he did so, the Prophet (ﷺ) got up as if he had been released from being tied up.[207]

Every nation on Earth has records of people who have practised some form of magic. Although some of it may have been false, it is highly unlikely that the whole of mankind could have agreed to make up similar stories about magical and supernatural events. Anyone who seriously contemplates the widespread presence of recorded instances of supernatural phenomena, will conclude that there must be some common thread of reality to them. "Haunted" houses, seances, ouija boards, voodoo, demonic-possession, speaking in tongues, levitation, etc., all represent puzzles to those unfamiliar with the world of the *Jinn*. All of these occurrences have their own manifestations in various parts of the world. Even the Muslim world is plagued with it, especially, among the shaykhs

---

[206] Deuteronomy 18:9-12.

[207] Collected by 'Abd ibn Ḥumayd and al-Bayhaqī and much of it can also be found in *al-Bukhārī* (*Ṣaḥīḥ Al-Bukhārī* (Arabic-English), vol. 7, pp. 443-4, no. 660) and *Muslim* (*Ṣaḥīḥ Muslim* (English Trans.), vol. 3, pp. 1192-3, no. 5428.

(masters) of various extremist *Ṣūfī* (mystical) orders. Many of them appear to levitate, travel huge distances in split instants of time, produce food or money from nowhere, etc. Their ignorant followers believe these feats of magic to be divine miracles and thus, willingly give their wealth and lives in service to their shaykhs. But behind all of these phenomena lie the hidden and sinister world of the *Jinn*.

Although the *Jinn* are essentially invisible except for those in the snake and dog form,[208] some of them are able to take any form they wish including human form. For example, Abū Hurayrah said, *"Allāh's messenger made me responsible to protect the Zakāh (charity) of Ramaḍān. While I was doing so, someone came and began to dig around in the food so I caught a hold of him. I said, 'By Allāh I am going to take you to Allāh's messenger!' The man implored, 'Verily I am poor and I have dependants. I am in great need.' So I let him go. The next morning, the Prophet (ﷺ) said, 'O Abū Hurayrah, what did your captive do last night?' I said, 'He complained of being in great need and of having a family so I let him go.' The Prophet (ﷺ) replied, 'Surely he lied to you and he will return.' Since I knew that he was going to return, I laid in wait for him. When he returned and began to dig in the food, I grabbed him and said, 'I'm definitely going to take you to Allāh's messenger.' He pleaded, 'Let me go! Verily I'm poor and I do have a family. I won't return.' So I had mercy on him and let him go. The next morning Allāh's messenger said, 'O Abū Hurayrah, what did your captive do last night?' I said that he complained of being in great need and of having a family, so I let him go. The Prophet (ﷺ) replied, 'Surely he lied to you and he will return.' So I waited for him and grabbed him when he began to scatter the food around. I said, 'By Allāh, I will take you to Allāh's messenger. This is the third time, and you promised you would not return. Yet you came back anyway!' He said, 'Let me give you some words by which Allāh will benefit you.'*

---

[208] See chapter five on fortune-tellers, pp. 76-7, for evidence of this fact.

I said, "What are they?' He replied, 'Whenever you go to bed recite Āyāt ul-Kursī[209] *from beginning to end. If you do so, a guardian from Allāh will always be with you and Satan will not come near you until the morning.' Then I let him go. The next morning Allāh's messenger said, What did your captive do last night?' I said that he claimed that he would teach me some words by which Allāh would benefit me so I let him go. When the Prophet (ﷺ) asked what they were, I told him that they were saying Āyāt ul-Kursī before going to bed. I also told him that he said that a guardian from Allāh would remain with me and Satan would not come near me until I awoke in the morning. The Prophet (ﷺ) said, 'Surely he has told the truth although he is a compulsive liar. O, Abū Hurayrah! Do you know who you have been speaking to these past three nights?' I replied, 'No'. And he said, 'That was a devil.'"*[210]

Since both the practice and learning of magic is classified in Islām as *Kufr* (disbelief), the *Sharī'ah* (law) has set aside a very stiff sentence for anyone caught practising it. The penalty for anyone caught practising it, who does not repent and give it up, is death. This law is based on the following *Ḥadīth* reported by Jundub ibn Ka'b: The companions of the Prophet (ﷺ) said, "*The prescribed punishment for the magician is that he be executed by the sword.*"[211] This law was applied vigorously by the Righteous caliphs who led the Muslim nation after the Prophet's (ﷺ) death. Bajālah ibn

---

[209] Verse number 255 of Sūrah *al-Baqarah* (2).

[210] Collected by al-Bukhārī (*Ṣaḥīḥ Al-Bukhāri,* (Arabic-English), vol. 9, pp. 491-2, no. 530).

[211] Collected by *al-Tirmidhī*. This *Ḥadīth,* though *Ḍa'īf* (weak) in its chain of narration has been upgraded to the level of *Ḥasan,* (relatively authentic) due to supporting evidence. Three of the leading four legists (Aḥmad, Abū Ḥanīfah and Mālik) ruled according to it, while the fourth, al-Shāfi'i ruled that the magician should only be killed if his magic feats reached the level of *Kufr* (see *Taysīr al-'Azīz al-Ḥamīd,* pp. 390-91).

ʿAbdah reported that Caliph ʿUmar ibn al-Khaṭṭāb sent a letter to the Muslim forces waging a compaign against Rome and Persia which commanded them to inform all the Zoroastrians married to their mothers, daughters and sisters to dissolve such marriages. They were also told to eat the food of Zoroastrians in order to include them in the category of "*Ahl-al-Kitāb*."[212] Finally, *they were ordered to kill every fortune-teller and magician whom they found.* Bajālah said that on the basis of the order, he personally executed three magicians.[213] This punishment is also recorded in the Torah to this day, clearly showing the Jews and Christians that magic is forbidden: "A man or a woman who is a medium or a wizard shall be put to death; they shall be stoned with stones, their blood shall be put upon them."[214]

The severity of the ruling on magicians is primarily to protect the weaker elements of society from falling into idolatry (*shirk*) by attributing to magicians divine qualities belonging only to Allāh. In addition to the sacrilege committed by those who practise witchcraft in earnest, magicians often claim for themselves supernatural powers and divine attributes, in order to attract a following and earn undue fame.

Demonic Possession

Jinns are also able to travel over vast distances instantaneously and enter objects as well as human bodies prepared for their entry. Allāh has seen fit to give them these extraordinary abilities, as He has given other creatures abilities beyond those of man. Yet, He has chosen man to be above all of creation. If these basic facts about the *Jinn's* abilities are kept in mind, all of the supernatural and

---

[212] Those who follow a revealed scripture like the Jews and Christians. This portion of the narration was collected by *al-Bukhārī*, *al-Tirmidhī* and *al Nasā'ī*.

[213] Collected by *Aḥmad*, *Abū Dāwūd* and *al-Bayhaqī*.

[214] Leviticus 20:27.

magical incidents which are not hoaxes can be easily explained. For example, in the cases of "haunted" houses, where lights go on and off, pictures fall from the walls, objects fly through the air, floors creak, etc., the *Jinns* are acting on material objects while remaining in their invisible form. This is also true in the case of seances where the spirits of dead people seemingly communicate with the living. People who know the voices of their dead relatives, hear them speak to them of incidents from their lives. This feat is accomplished by the medium summoning the *Jinn* which was assigned to the dead person. It is this *Jinn* which imitates the dead person's voice and relates incidents from the person's past. This is also true in the case of the ouija board which appears to answer questions. The invisible prodding of the *Jinn* can easily cause amazing results if the proper atmosphere is set. In the case of those who appear to be able to levitate or raise objects without touching them, they are simply lifted up into the air by the invisible hand of the *Jinn*. Those able to travel vast distances and be in two places at almost the same time are transported by their invisible companions or the *Jinn* may even become visible in their form. Likewise, those like Sai Baba who are able to produce food or money from the air are aided by the invisible and fast moving *Jinn*.[215] Even the most amazing cases of apparent reincarnation occur like that of a seven year old girl in India by the name of Shanti Devi who related instances from her previous life in vivid and accurate detail. She described her former home in the town of Muttra which was in a province far away from where she lived. When people went there to check, the local people confirmed that such a house had once stood where she described. They also confirmed some of the details of her former life.[216] This information was put into her

---

[215] See *Ibn Taymiyyah's Essay on the Jinn,* pp. 47-59, for numerous accounts of such incidences.

[216] Colin Wilson, *The Occult,* (New York: Random House, 1971), pp. 514-15.

subconscious mind by the *Jinn*. The Prophet (ﷺ) confirmed this phenomena when he said, "*Verily the dreams which a man sees in his sleep are of three types: A dream from al-Raḥmān (Allāh), a sad dream from Satan and subconscious dreams.*"[217]

The *Jinn* can also enter the human body as it enters the mind. Cases of possession are too numerous to count. It may be temporary as in the case of many Christian and pagan sects where people work themselves into a physical and spiritual frenzy, fall into a state of unconsciousness and begin to speak in foreign tongues. In that weakened state, the *Jinn* may easily enter their bodies and cackle on their lips. This phenomena has also been recorded by some*Ṣūfi*[218] orders during their *Dhikr*[219] sessions. Or, it may be a long term phenomenon wherein major personality changes take place. The possessed often act irrationally, exhibit superhuman strength or the *Jinn* may actually talk through them on a regular basis.

Exorcism[220] became a widespread practice in Europe during the middle ages. The Christian practice of exorcism is based on numerous accounts of Jesus exorcising possessed people as related in the Gospels. In one account, Jesus and his companions came to Gerasenes and met a possessed man. When Jesus commanded the demons to leave him, they left him and entered a herd of swine which was feeding on a nearby hillside. The herd then rushed down the steep bank into the lake and were drowned.[221] It has also become the topic of a number of films produced in the late

---

[217] Reported by Abū Hurayrah and collected by Abū Dāwūd (*Sunan Abū Dāwūd,* (English Trans.), vol. 3, p. 1395, no. 5001).

[218] Mysticism which developed among Muslim peoples.

[219] God's names are repeated continuously and often musically while swaying the body or even dancing.

[220] The expulsion of evil spirits or demons from possessed people or places.

[221] See Matthew 8:28-34, Mark 5:1-20 and Luke 8:26-39.

seventies and eighties (e.g. "The Exorcist", "Rosemary's Baby", etc.). The general attitude of the materialist West is the rejection of everything supernatural. Thus, to Westerners, exorcism has no rational basis and is looked at as a result of superstition. This attitude is a reaction to the wide scale witch hunts and burnings which took place in Europe during the Dark and Middle ages. However, in Islām, the practice of exorcism is recognised as a valid means of treating genuine cases of possession and other ailments resulting from it, if the method conforms to the Qur'ān and the *Sunnah*.

There are essentially three methods of removing the *Jinn* from a possessed person:

1. The possessing *Jinn* may be removed by summoning another more powerful *Jinn*. This method is forbidden in Islām because calling the *Jinn* often involves acts of sacrilege. The tenets of Islām are likely to be desecrated for the *Jinn* to be beckoned. This is the case where a magician or witch breaks a spell cast by another.

2. The *Jinn* may be removed by confirming the symbols of idolatry in its presence. When the *Jinn* is satisfied by the idolatrous acts of the exorcist it may also leave. In doing so, he assures the exorcist that his method and beliefs are correct. This is the case of Christian priests who exorcise the *Jinn* by calling on Jesus and by using the cross, as well as that of pagan high priests who exorcise in the name of their false deities.

3. The *Jinn* may also be expelled by using Qur'ānic recitation and prayers seeking refuge in Allāh. These divine words and formulas help to change the atmosphere around the possessed. However, these practices by themselves are useless unless the one doing them has firm *Īmān* (faith) and a good contact with Allāh based on righteous deeds.

Although some Muslims today under Western secular influence openly deny possession and others even go so far as to deny the existence of the *Jinn*, both the Qur'ān and the *Sunnah* say otherwise. There are a number of authentic traditions in which the Prophet (ﷺ) is recorded as having exorcised people. There are, as well, traditions of his companions doing the same with his approval. Ya'lā ibn Murrah said, *"Once I went travelling with the Prophet (ﷺ) and we came across a woman sitting with her child in the road. She said, 'O messenger of Allāh, this boy has been afflicted and has caused us many trials. I don't know how many times per day he is seized by spells!' The Prophet (ﷺ) said, 'Give him to me.' So she raised him up to him and the Prophet (ﷺ) put the boy in front of him in the middle of his saddle. Then he opened the boy's mouth, blew*[222] *in it thrice and said, 'Bismillāh (in the name of Allāh)! I am a slave of Allāh, so get away, o enemy of Allāh!' Then he returned the boy to the woman, and said, 'Meet us here on our return and tell us what happened.' Then we went and on our return we found her at the place. She had with her three sheep so the Prophet (ﷺ) asked, 'How is your boy?' She replied, 'By the One who has sent you with the truth, we haven't noticed anything wrong with him since then, so I've brought you these sheep.' The Prophet (ﷺ) said to me, 'Dismount and take one. Then return the rest to her.'*[223]

Khārijah ibn al-Ṣalt reported that his uncle said, *"Once, when we left Allāh's messenger's company, we came across a bedouin tribe. Some of them said, 'We have been told that you have come with some good things from that man (i.e.Prophet Muḥammad). Do you have any medicine or incantation for a possessed man?' We answered yes, so they brought a madman bound in a spell. I recited the Fātiḥa over him*

---

[222] The Arabic word used here is نفث (*Nafatha*) which means to put the tip of the tongue between the lips and blow. It is thus a cross between blowing (*Nafakha*) and spitting lightly (*Tafala*).

[223] Collected by Aḥmad.

every morning and evening for three days. Every time I completed the recitation, I would gather my saliva and spit. Finally he got up as if he broke free from being tied in bonds. The Bedouins then brought me a gift as payment, so I said to them, 'I can't accept in until I ask Allāh's messenger.' When I asked the Prophet, he said, 'Take it. For, by my life, whoever eats by way of false incantations will bear the burden of his sin. But you have earned that wage with an incantation of truth.'"[224]

The main characteristic that belief in the *jinn* builds is:

A cautious personality

Knowledge of the world of the *jinn* protects humans from falling into their traps. It provides the believers with a firm basis for understanding 'supernatural' events which may occur in their world, without resorting to beliefs and acts of *shirk* (idolatry).

III. Belief in the Books

1. Belief in the Books refers to the concept that God revealed His word to humankind in scriptures. Books of revelation were given to human beings from the time of Ādam to the last of the prophets of God, Muḥammad. Specific reference is made in the Qur'ān to the scripture given to Prophet Abraham, the *Torah* given to Prophet Moses, the *Psalms* revealed to Prophet David, the *Gospel* bestowed on Prophet Jesus and the *Qur'ān* given to Prophet Muḥammad.

2. Belief in the Books means accepting the scriptures named in the Qur'ān as well as accepting that other

[224] Collected by Abū Dāwūd (*Sunan Abū Dāwūd* (English Trans.), vol. 3, p. 1092, no. 3887).

scriptures whose names are not mentioned in the Qur'ān were also revealed to other prophets. However, all of these scriptures have either been totally lost, or become so distorted over the ages, that the existing books carrying these names cannot be considered to be the revealed books of God. Some of the existing scriptures followed by Jews and Christians contain portions of God's revelation, but much of these books are the products of human tampering. Due to the fact that they do contain some portions of revelation, God afforded them special status by mentioning them by name in the Qur'ān and requiring Muslims to believe in their original versions.

3. Belief in the Books also includes believing that the Qur'ān was the last revealed scripture to humankind, that it was preserved in its original form and that every single word in the Qur'ān is the word of God. Modern scriptural research which confirms that the Old and New Testaments have been modified also confirms that the Arabic Qur'ān available today was that taught by Prophet Muḥammad.

The main character built by belief in the divine scriptures is that of thankfulness.

The believers should have a thankful nature, willingly showing gratitude to whomsoever does good for them. The Books represent a special gift granted by God to human beings. God gave every created soul a consciousness of good and evil and could have left them with that alone to guide them to righteousness. The scripture is a bonus given to humans to remind themselves of the correct way. God speaks to humans through His scriptures. Giving thanks to God is a fundamental part of worship. Consequently, the Muslim five-times daily prayer begins with the phrase : *Al-hamdu lil-lāhi rabbil-'ālamīn* [All praise and thanks belongs to Allāh, Lord of all the worlds]. The believer gives thanks to Allāh for all of the various favours and mercies in his or her life. Thankfulness to God creates a positive attitude towards God. The believers should not allow success to make them forget God. The Prophet's companion, Ṣuhayb ibn Sinān, quoted him as saying, "*The affair of the believer is amazing! The whole of his life is beneficial, and that is only in the case of the believer. When good times come to him, he is thankful and it is good for him, and when bad times befall him, he is patient and it is also good for him.*"[225] Furthermore, even in the worst of times, the believer is encouraged to give thanks to God by considering the state of others less fortunate. Prophet Muḥammad advised his followers saying, "*Look to those less fortunate than you, and do not look to those above you; it is better for you, in order that you not deny what Allāh has blessed you with.*"[226] Thankfulness helps to create a sense of balance in the believer's life. It creates a sense of responsibility for others, since whatever good one has is from God. On the other hand, ingratitude ultimately leads to corruption and excesses. When people feel that whatever good they are favoured with is their own to use as they wish, it is very easy for them to squander their wealth.

God also encouraged the believers to be thankful saying: "If you are thankful, I will certainly increase [my favour on] you."[227]

The quality of gratitude also extends to other human beings. The Prophet was reported to have said, "*Whoever does not give thanks to people, does not give thanks to Allāh.*"[228] It is true that

---

[225] *Ṣaḥīḥ Muslim,* vol. 4, p. 1541, no. 7138.

[226] *Ṣaḥīḥ al Bukhāri,* vol. 8, p. 328, no. 497 and *Ṣaḥīḥ Muslim,* vol. 4, p. 1530, no. 7070.

[227] Sūrah *Ibrāhīm* (14):7.

[228] Collected by Aḥmad and al-Tirmidhi.

whatever good people do is by the will of God, thus all good ultimately comes from God. However, the intermediaries whom God chose to bring good also played an active role and, thus, gratitude should also be shown to them. Giving thanks to people encourages people to continue to do good. When people are helpful and their efforts go unthanked, scorned or unnoticed, they usually become discouraged and reluctant to do the same again.

IV. Belief in the Messengers

1. Belief in the messengers of God fundamentally means believing that God communicated His message to humankind through other human beings. Allāh chose certain human beings and made them superior to the rest of humankind by communicating directly to them and by making them examples to the rest of humanity. Allāh stated in the Qur'ān, "I preferred all of them over the worlds [of man and *jinn*]."[229] The prophets demonstrated how God's message was to be implemented. They were not like postmen, merely delivering letters to others, without any relationship to the contents of the letters.

2. Belief that the messengers were specially chosen by the Creator requires that Muslims reject the stories of corruption attributed to the prophets in the distortions of the earlier scriptures presently circulating among the Christians and Jews. The prophets are depicted in the Old Testament as drunkards,[230] committing

---

[229] Sūrah *al-An'ām*, (6):86. See also Sūrah *Āl 'Imrān* (3):33.

[230] Prophet Noah [Genesis 9:21].

incest[231] and adultery,[232] patronizing prostitutes,[233] and worshipping idols.[234] Such slander and abuse of the prophets has to be opposed for belief in the messengers to be complete. The prophets were guides to righteousness and not guides to corruption. The Qur'ān restores the prophets to their honoured position of guides for humankind and corrects the false claims attributed to them. For example, Allāh mentions a discussion which He will have with Prophet Jesus on the Day of Judgement to refute the claim that Prophet Jesus invited people to worship him, "When Allāh will say: O Jesus, son of Mary, did you tell people to worship you and your mother as gods besides Allāh? He will reply, 'Glory be to You. It was not fitting for me to say what I had no right to say.... I never said to them anything but what You commanded me to say: Worship Allāh, my Lord and your Lord.'"[235] From the Islamic perspective, the claim that Jesus demanded that his followers worship him is, in fact, an even greater lie than the false stories of moral corruption attributed by the Jews to the earlier prophets. To worship anyone besides God is considered the greatest of all sins. All sins may be forgiven by God if one dies without repenting from them except *shirk*. Allāh said in the Qur'ān: "Surely

---

[231] Prophet Lot with his daughters [Genesis 19:30] and Prophet David's son with his sister [2 Samuel 13:1].

[232] Judah with his daughter-in-law [Genesis 38:15], David with his neighbour's wife [2 Samuel 11:1].

[233] God tells Hosea to choose a harlot wife [Hosea 1:2].

[234] Prophet Solomon worshipped idols [1 King 11:3].

[235] Sūrah *al-Mā'idah*, (5):116-7.

Allāh will not forgive the association of partners (*shirk*) with Him, but He forgives [sins] less than that of whomever He wishes."[236]

3. Belief in the messengers also means believing that Allāh sent messengers to all the nations, the first of whom was Ādam and the last, Muḥammad. Allāh stated in the Qur'ān, "I have sent among every nation a messenger."[237] Muslims must believe in all of the prophets whose names were mentioned in the Qur'ān as well as others whose names were not mentioned. As to those mentioned in the Old Testament, since the text has been tampered with, no one can say with certainty that they were prophets. Likewise, Muslims cannot accept Buddha or Zoroaster as prophets, nor would they deny the possibility that they may have been prophets whose messages were distorted after their deaths. Regarding the unmentioned prophets, Allāh said, "And indeed I have sent messengers before you. Some of them I have related to you their story while others I have not."[238]

4. Belief that messengers were sent by God also means accepting that the essence of their messages was one. Consequently, God's religion is only one. There is only one God, one race of human beings and one religion. In this regard, Allāh said in the Qur'ān, "I have sent among every nation a messenger [proclaiming]: Worship Allāh alone and avoid all

---

236 Sūrah *al-Nisā'*, (4):48.

237 Sūrah *al-Naḥl*, (16):36.

238 Sūrah *Ghāfir*, (40):78.

false gods."[239] God did not communicate different messages to different generations and nations of humans; some He told to worship stars and planets, others He told to worship trees, animals and human beings and yet others He told that the worship of His creation is the greatest of evils. To accept all religions as being from God is to accept that God is the author of confusion. The fact is that it is God alone who answers prayers, thus it is He alone who deserves the worship of humans. This was the essence of the message which all the prophets of God brought.

The character that belief in divinely sent messengers builds is:

a) a questioning character.

1. The believer's character is not one which blindly submits itself to other human beings, customs or to fashion. Traditionalism and custom demand from the members of society blind obedience. Members of the community are not allowed to challenge the customs with regard to their rightness or wrongness. Customs are to be followed because they were inherited from the community's ancestors. To reject the practice of the foreparents, is to reject the fore parents and to disgrace them. Consequently, the upholders of tradition do not tolerate any challenge to their traditional practices. On the other hand, believers are required to judge all customary practices according to the teachings of the Qur'ān and the Sunnah of the Prophet. Those practices which do not contradict the revelation are acceptable, and those which do are not.

[239]. Sūrah *al-Naḥl*, (16):36.

2. Believers do not follow any individual blindly, no matter how pious they may seem. All human beings are prone to making mistakes. Only the prophets were divinely protected from mistakes which would lead to misguidance. This is the reason why their followers were obliged to follow them as an article of faith in God. In order to oblige people to follow other human beings, incredible stories are invented, either by those who demand blind following of themselves or by their henchmen. The stories usually involve attributing to them either supernatural abilities and or divine qualities. For example, Twelver Shi'ites believe that eleven of the Prophet's grandchildren, who along with his son-in-law are referred to as "the twelve Imāms", were infallible, omniscient and omnipotent. Followers of the Agha Khan, known as a branch of the Ismā'ili Shi'ites, believe that Agha Khan is God incarnate.

3. The believer is also not a slave to fashion. Being "in", "with it", or fashionable is not the basic code of the believer. The Prophet had said, "*The believer is not malleable; when the people are righteous he is righteous, and when they are corrupt he is corrupt.*" The believer would not change his or her wardrobe every spring, summer and fall in order to keep up with the latest styles, because that would require extravagance. Clothes would be cast aside, simply because they were out of fashion and new clothes bought. Allāh expressed his dislike for extravagance in the Qur'ān saying, "Verily the squanderers are brethren of the devils, and the devil was a disbeliever in his Lord."[240]

---

[240] Sūrah *al-Isrā'*, (17):27.

> Nor would the believer wear any style, simply because it was fashionable. If the style contradicted explicit commandments of the Prophet regarding dress, the believer would avoid it. Otherwise, the fashion or sunnah of the society would then become more pleasing to the Muslim than the Sunnah of the Prophet. When a person reaches that state, he or she has abandoned the community of believers. The Prophet was quoted by his companion Ibn 'Umar as saying, "*Whoever imitates a people is of them.*"[241]

b) a devoutly obedient character

Belief in the messengers, reinforces obedience to God. By psychologically training the believers to obey the messengers because they were sent by God, this pillar of faith inculcates in the mind of the believer a desire to obey the Creator.

c) a thankful character

Belief in the messengers, like belief in the scriptures, helps to develop the quality of gratitude in the true believer. Allāh could have miraculously revealed the scriptures without sending prophets, since the books were already an additional favour to humans over and above the spiritual consciousness of good and evil with which Allāh created every human being. However, some people might have claimed that it was not humanly possible to follow the divine injunctions in the Books, and others may have engaged in personal interpretations of the scriptures which would suit their own fancies. Consequently, sending prophets from among the various nations to demonstrate how the scriptures were to be implemented was an additional favour from God for which humans should always be grateful.

---

[241] Collected by Abū Dāwūd and authenticated in *Ṣaḥīḥ al-Jāmi' al-Ṣaghīr,* vol. 2, no. 6149.

V. Belief in the Last Day

1. Belief in the Last Day means belief in an end to this world when humankind will be resurrected. It is belief that when a person dies, he or she will not return to this life. There is a barrier, known as the *Barzakh*, behind everyone whose soul leaves this life preventing them from returning until the time of resurrection. At the appointed time of resurrection, Allāh will command all of the atoms which once constituted human bodies to reassemble along with their souls, and human beings will once again be completely alive. It is thus, in clear opposition to the belief in re-incarnation.

2. Belief in the Last Day also means belief in the Judgement. All human beings who ever lived on the earth will be judged by God. Their lives will be reviewed and their deeds weighed. In the judgement of mankind at the end of this world, God's attributes of supreme justice and fairness become manifest. Based on His infinite knowledge, God could have created all members of the human race who were to live on earth and immediately placed some of them in paradise and the remainder in hell. Before creating man, Allāh already knew what choices they would make in this life, what provision and opportunities He would give them, and in what state of belief or disbelief they would die. Therefore, in one sense it could be said that some people were created for paradise and others for hell. 'Ā'ishah (ﷺ), wife of the Prophet Muḥammad (ﷺ), quoted him as saying, "*Don't you know that Allāh created paradise and hell,*

and He created inhabitants for each?"[242] If God had immediately placed those headed for paradise in paradise, they would not question His decision. Those in paradise would happily accept an everlasting life of bliss and be thankful that they were not placed in hell. However, those immediately placed in hell would ask why. They would feel a sense of unfairness due to their ignorance of what they would have done had they lived on earth. Those in hell would relentlessly argue that had they been given a chance to live out their lives on earth, they would have believed and done righteous deeds. Consequently, Allāh allows human beings to live out their lives on earth and make all the choices they would have made, so that everyone who enters hell will know that they chose hell by themselves. They will recognise God's mercy in their lives and acknowledge their sin in rejecting His signs and guidance. And they will accept His judgement as being just and beyond reproach. Instead of arguing with God, they will beg for another chance to do good in this world, as God says in chapter *al-Sajdah* of the Qur'ān:

وَلَوْ تَرَىٰٓ إِذِ ٱلْمُجْرِمُونَ نَاكِسُوا۟ رُءُوسِهِمْ عِندَ رَبِّهِمْ
رَبَّنَآ أَبْصَرْنَا وَسَمِعْنَا فَٱرْجِعْنَا نَعْمَلْ صَٰلِحًا إِنَّا مُوقِنُونَ ﴿١٢﴾

"If only you could see [the time] when the sinners will bow their heads before their Lord [saying], 'Our Lord! We have now seen and heard, so send us back and we will do righteous deeds. Verily, we now believe with certainty.'" Sūrah *al-Sajdah* (32):12.

[242] *Ṣaḥīḥ Muslim,* vol. 4, p. 1400, no. 6435.

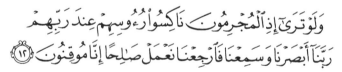

However, if Allāh were to send them back to this world having forgotten what they had seen of hell, they would again choose evil and end up in hell as before. God spoke about this in chapter *al-An'ām*:

وَلَوْ رُدُّوا۟ لَعَادُوا۟ لِمَا نُهُوا۟ عَنْهُ وَإِنَّهُمْ لَكَٰذِبُونَ

"But if they were returned [to this world], they would certainly go back to what was forbidden to them. Indeed they are liars." Sūrah *al-An'ām* (6):28.

3. Belief in the Last Day includes belief in the consequence of the Judgement: Heaven and Hell. Those whose good deeds outweigh their evil deeds, will be sent to paradise and those whose evil deeds outweigh their good deeds will be sent to hell. It should be noted that it is by people's deeds and God's grace that anyone will enter paradise. The Prophet (ﷺ) was quoted as saying, "*Observe moderation, but if you fail, try to do as much as you can moderately, and be happy. For, none will enter paradise only because of his deeds.*" The [companions of the Prophet] asked, "O Messenger of Allāh! Not even you?" He replied, "*Not even I, were it not that Allāh enveloped me in His mercy and grace.*[243] *And bear in mind that the deed most loved by Allāh is one done constantly, even though it is small.*"[244] However, God's grace is not arbitrary. It is based on both correct faith and righteous deeds. In chapter *Āl 'Imrān*, Allāh says:

مَن جَآءَ بِٱلْحَسَنَةِ فَلَهُۥ عَشْرُ أَمْثَالِهَا ۖ وَمَن جَآءَ بِٱلسَّيِّئَةِ

[243] *Ṣaḥīḥ Muslim,* vol. 4, p. 1473, no. 6765, reported by Abū Hurayrah.

[244] *Ṣaḥīḥ Muslim,* vol. 4, pp. 1473-4, no. 6770, reported by 'Ā'ishah.

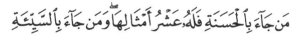

فَلَا يُجْزَىٰٓ إِلَّا مِثْلَهَا وَهُمْ لَا يُظْلَمُونَ ﴿١٦٠﴾

> "Whoever brings a good deed, shall have [the value of] ten like it, and whoever brings an evil deed will only be punished with one like it, and they will not be wronged." Sūrah *Al-ʿImrān* (6):160.

Were God to hold humankind to account strictly, no one's good deeds would outweigh their evil deeds. However, God has manifested His grace by multiplying the value of good deeds, while keeping evil deeds at their face value. Furthermore, the Prophet (ﷺ) had stated, "*Indeed Allāh has recorded all good and evil. Then He explained that whoever intended good but did not do it would have one complete good deed recorded on his behalf. If he intended good and did it, Allāh would record ten to seven hundred good deeds for him. If he intended evil but did not do it, one complete good deed would also be recorded for him. And if he intended evil and did it, Allāh would only record a single evil deed against him.*"[245] Thus, it is ultimately by the grace of God that the true believers enter Paradise. Deeds have a major role since God's grace is connected to them, but they are not the deciding factor. God's grace outweighs them. Consequently, the creation of human beings, the errors that they make, the good that they do, are all circumstances for the manifestation of God's attributes of mercy and forgiveness, His attribute of justice and His attribute of grace.

Those humans whose evil deeds outweigh their good deeds will be sent to Hell. However, anyone who truly believed in God in this life will ultimately be removed from the Hellfire and placed in paradise. Those who rejected God and disbelieved in His messengers will remain eternally in Hell.

---

[245] *Ṣaḥīḥ al Bukhāri,* vol. 8, p. 329, no. 498 and *Ṣaḥīḥ Muslim,* vol. 1, pp. 75-6, no. 237.

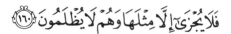

The character that belief in the Resurrection and Judgement builds is:

a) a calculating personality

Those who believe in the After-life, resurrection and judgement, are obliged to consider carefully the consequence of their deeds. Belief in the Last Day causes them to think beyond their immediate needs and desires. It sets their goals beyond this temporal existence.

Consequently, the Prophet (ﷺ) often connected righteous deeds with belief in the Last Day. For example, he was reported to have said, "*Whoever believes in Allāh and the Last Day should either speak good or be silent.*" On another occasion he was quoted as saying, "*Whoever believes in Allāh and the Last Day should be kind to his guest.*"

b) a firm, uncompromising personality

Believers in the Judgement will not compromise the basic commandments of God in order to attain some limited measure of material success. They will be principled individuals, sticking by their beliefs and practices regardless of how odd they may seem or how lonely and isolated the society may make them. Allāh said, "Say: The evil and the good are not equal, even though the abundance of evil may amaze you."[246]

Those who do not believe in the Judgement tend to be good as long as it is convenient. But when everyone else around them are cheating or stealing, or being honest will cost economic loss, they usually compromise their principles with appropriate justifications.

c) a confident personality

Belief in the Last Day reassures the believers that no matter how successful corrupt people may appear in this life, they are ultimately failures. Allāh said,

---

[246] Sūrah *al-Mā'idah*, (5):100.

فَلَا تُعْجِبْكَ أَمْوَٰلُهُمْ وَلَآ أَوْلَـٰدُهُمْ ۚ إِنَّمَا يُرِيدُ ٱللَّهُ لِيُعَذِّبَهُم
بِهَا فِى ٱلْحَيَوٰةِ ٱلدُّنْيَا وَتَزْهَقَ أَنفُسُهُمْ وَهُمْ كَـٰفِرُونَ ﴿٥٥﴾

> "Do not let their wealth and children amaze you. It is Allāh's plan to punish them with these things in this life and let their souls leave while they are disbelievers." Sūrah *al-Tawbah*, (9): 55.

Those without belief in the Judgement are easily tempted into evil because they have no real confidence in the ultimate superiority of good over evil. They may espouse good for good's sake while they experience some measure of success in life, but as soon as upholding good brings about their failure, and those who are corrupt around them succeed, they immediately question, "What is the point?" or "Why bother?"

VI. Belief in the Destiny

Belief in *Qadar* (Destiny or fate) is the sixth pillar of *Īmān* (faith) which Angel Gabriel received in Prophet Muḥammad's answer to his question about *Īmān*. Belief in destiny is a very important part of faith. However, people have argued in ignorance about destiny from the most ancient times. They argued about it even in the time of Prophet Muḥammad (ﷺ) and continue to do so until today. Within the context of Islamic teaching, the truth regarding *Qadar* is so clear that there is no need for any argumentation or disagreement.

Belief in *Qadar* means accepting that Allāh has predestined everything. Allāh stated in Sūrah *al-Qamar* (54):49 of the Qur'ān:

إِنَّا كُلَّ شَىْءٍ خَلَقْنَـٰهُ بِقَدَرٍ ﴿٤٩﴾

"Indeed, I have created everything preordained."

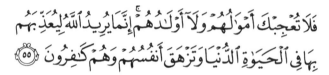

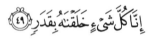

That is, Allāh created everything and predetermined its measure or destined its reality. The destiny which Allāh has set for things is consistent with His wisdom, on the basis of which He created all things. It is consistent with the goals and benefits which Allāh intends for His creatures.

Belief in destiny is comprised of four (4) basic principles:

The First Principle: Knowledge (*ʿIlm*)

That is, to believe absolutely, that Allāh's knowledge encompasses all things. Nothing is outside of His knowledge. Nothing of the past, the present or the future is unknown to the Creator. Whether the knowledge is related to the actions or deeds of God, or whether it is related to the deeds of His creatures, it is all the same to God. His knowledge is not limited to the broad outlines of what will happen in history, but includes detailed knowledge of the minutest actions of every individual. The Divine attributes are infinite: without beginning and without end. Consequently, Allāh's knowledge is without limits. This principle of boundless knowledge is mentioned in numerous verses of the Qur'ān. For example, Allāh said the following in Sūrah *Āl ʿImrān* (3):5:

إِنَّ ٱللَّهَ لَا يَخْفَىٰ عَلَيْهِ شَىْءٌ فِى ٱلْأَرْضِ وَلَا فِى ٱلسَّمَآءِ ۝٥

> "Indeed, nothing in the earth or in the skies is hidden from Allāh."

There is nothing in creation unknown to God. The earth and skies, relative to humans, represent the totality of creation. In Sūrah *al-Anʿām* (6):59, Allāh states:

۞ وَعِندَهُۥ مَفَاتِحُ ٱلْغَيْبِ لَا يَعْلَمُهَآ إِلَّا هُوَ

> "He has with Him the keys to the unknown and only He knows them."

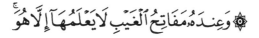

All that is unperceived by creation, due to the limitations of their senses of perception, is known to Allāh. To claim that there are some aspects of knowledge unknown to God is to deny this principle and attribute falsehood to Allāh and His messengers. It also involves denying the perfection of Allāh, because the opposite of knowledge is either ignorance or forgetfulness, both of which cannot be attributed to Allāh.

When Pharaoh asked Prophet Moses:

قَالَ فَمَن رَّبُّكُمَا يَٰمُوسَىٰ ﴿٤٩﴾

> "Who then, O Moses, is the Lord of you [and Aaron]?" Sūrah *Ṭā-Hā* (20):49.

He replied that his Lord was the Creator:

قَالَ رَبُّنَا ٱلَّذِىٓ أَعْطَىٰ كُلَّ شَىْءٍ خَلْقَهُۥ ثُمَّ هَدَىٰ ﴿٥٠﴾

> "Our Lord is the one who gives each and everything its shape and then guides it." Sūrah *Ṭā-Hā* (20):50.

Pharaoh then asked:

قَالَ فَمَا بَالُ ٱلْقُرُونِ ٱلْأُولَىٰ ﴿٥١﴾

> "What about the previous generations?" Sūrah *Ṭā-Hā* (20): 51.

Mūsā's reply was:

قَالَ عِلْمُهَا عِندَ رَبِّى فِى كِتَٰبٍ ۖ لَّا يَضِلُّ رَبِّى وَلَا يَنسَى ﴿٥٢﴾

> "Knowledge about them is with my Lord (recorded) in a book; my Lord neither errs nor forgets." Sūrah *Ṭā-Hā* (20): 52.

That knowledge of the earlier generations is with the Lord means that the past is known to God. When one has forgotten things which have taken place, he makes mistakes. Similarly, when one is ignorant of something in the future, one may also err. Consequently, Prophet Mūsā reaffirmed Allāh's infinite knowledge.

Second Principle: The Writing

This principle begins with the belief that Allāh has recorded the destiny of all things that exist, will exist or have existed until the last hour and beyond. When Allāh created the pen, as was reported by Prophet Muḥammad (ﷺ) in a ḥadīth, He instructed it to write, and the pen asked what it should write, whereupon Allāh told it to write everything that was and would be. Not only the generalities but the fine details have been recorded and preserved. Evidence of these can be found in the verse:

أَلَمْ تَعْلَمْ أَنَّ ٱللَّهَ يَعْلَمُ مَا فِى ٱلسَّمَآءِ وَٱلْأَرْضِ ۗ إِنَّ ذَٰلِكَ
فِى كِتَٰبٍ ۚ إِنَّ ذَٰلِكَ عَلَى ٱللَّهِ يَسِيرٌ ﴿٧٠﴾

"Don't you know that Allāh knows all that is in the heaven and the earth, indeed, it is all in a book, and indeed that is easy for Allāh." Sūrah *al-Ḥajj* (22):70.

In the case of the developing foetus, after four months have passed, an angel is sent to record four things: how long that child will live, what provision it will have in life, its deeds and whether it will be wretched or happy.[247] It was reported in a ḥadīth that on the night of power (*Laylāt al Qadr*), the deeds or the events of the coming year are recorded, as in the verse:

إِنَّآ أَنزَلْنَٰهُ فِى لَيْلَةٍ
مُّبَٰرَكَةٍ ۚ إِنَّا كُنَّا مُنذِرِينَ ﴿٣﴾ فِيهَا يُفْرَقُ كُلُّ أَمْرٍ حَكِيمٍ ﴿٤﴾

"Surely, I revealed it on a blessed night - surely I am always warning - during it every wise affair is made distinct." Sūrah *al-Dukhān* (44):3-4.

---

[247] *Ṣaḥīḥ Muslim*, 4:1391, no. 6390.

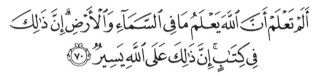

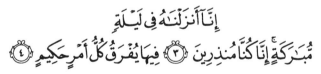

The Third Principle: Accordance with Allāh's Will

Everything which has taken place in creation happens according to Allāh's will, whether it is a result of Allāh's action or what is done by humans. Allāh said:

أَلَمْ تَرَ أَنَّ ٱللَّهَ
يَسْجُدُ لَهُۥ مَن فِى ٱلسَّمَٰوَٰتِ وَمَن فِى ٱلْأَرْضِ وَٱلشَّمْسُ وَٱلْقَمَرُ
وَٱلنُّجُومُ وَٱلْجِبَالُ وَٱلشَّجَرُ وَٱلدَّوَآبُّ وَكَثِيرٌ مِّنَ ٱلنَّاسِ ۖ
وَكَثِيرٌ حَقَّ عَلَيْهِ ٱلْعَذَابُ ۗ وَمَن يُهِنِ ٱللَّهُ فَمَا لَهُۥ مِن مُّكْرِمٍ ۚ
إِنَّ ٱللَّهَ يَفْعَلُ مَا يَشَآءُ ۩ ﴿١٨﴾

Don't you see that all things in the heavens and on earth, the sun, the moon, the stars, the hills, the trees, the animals, and a great number among mankind bow down to Allāh in worship? But a great number are fit for punishment; and whoever Allāh disgraces, none can give him honour. Verily Allāh carries out all that He wills. Sūrah *al-Ḥajj* (22):18.

He also said that:

وَلَوْ شَآءَ لَهَدَىٰكُمْ أَجْمَعِينَ

"If He wished He would have guided all of you." Sūrah *al-Naḥl* (16):9.

He also said:

مَآ أَصَابَ مِن مُّصِيبَةٍ إِلَّا بِإِذْنِ ٱللَّهِ ۗ

"No calamity occurs except by Allāh's permission" Sūrah *al-Taghābun* (64):11.

Ibn ʿAbbās said "permission" here means "command." These and other verses show that whatever action of Allāh takes place is by His own wish and there are numbers of other verses which indicate that the actions of His creatures are in accordance with His will; for example:

إِنْ هُوَ إِلَّا ذِكْرٌ لِّلْعَٰلَمِينَ ﴿٢٧﴾ لِمَن شَآءَ مِنكُمْ أَن
يَسْتَقِيمَ ﴿٢٨﴾ وَمَا تَشَآءُونَ إِلَّآ أَن يَشَآءَ ٱللَّهُ رَبُّ ٱلْعَٰلَمِينَ ﴿٢٩﴾

> "Verily this is no less than a Message to (all) the worlds; to whoever among you wills to go straight: But you shall not will except as Allāh wills; the Lord of the Worlds." Sūrah *al-Takwīr* (81):27-29.

This clear evidence indicates that the actions of Allāh's creatures are according to Allāh's will. If Allāh did not wish them to act, the action wouldn't have occurred.

The Fourth Principle: Allāh has created everything.

Everything besides Him is created. The creation is Allāh's creation, and whatever is produced by them is also part of Allāh's creation, whether deeds or statements. They are all part of Allāh's creation, because the actions and statements of a human being are a part of his attributes. So if a human is created, then his attributes must also be created. Evidence of this can be found in Allāh's statement:

وَٱللَّهُ خَلَقَكُمْ وَمَا تَعْمَلُونَ ﴿٩٦﴾

> "Allāh created you and what you do." Sūrah *al-Ṣāffāt* (37): 96.

Allāh speaks about the creation of human beings and the creation of their deeds. Scholars have disagreed about the exact meaning of **ما** in this verse: is it **ما مصدرية** which would cause the verse to read: "Allāh created you and your actions," or is it **ما موصولة** which would make the verse mean "Allāh created you and what you do."

However, in either case they both indicate that Allāh has created the deeds of human beings. These four principles represent the different aspects of belief in destiny. One's belief in *qadar* is not complete unless each and every part is believed in.

It should be noted that belief in destiny does not negate the reality of cause and effect. The cause-and-effect system is itself destined or predetermined according to Allāh's will. God commanded us to do certain things which He has ordained. This will produce certain effects in accordance with the natural laws by which He runs the universe. An illustration of the correct understanding of this concept was provided when Caliph 'Umar was on his way to Syria and he was informed of a plague there. He took counsel from his companions, whether they should continue on their journey or return back to Madīnah, and they agreed to return back to Madīnah. When their decision was announced, Caliph 'Umar was asked, "How can you decide to go back to Madīnah? Are you fleeing from Allāh's destiny?" 'Umar responded نفر من قدر الله إلى قدر الله, "We are fleeing from Allāh's destiny to His destiny," i.e., to what He has destined. After that, 'Abdur-Raḥmān ibn 'Awf came and was informed about the situation, whereupon, he narrated a statement from Prophet Muḥammad (ﷺ) that if you hear that plague has descended on a place, you should not enter it. 'Umar's response when he was asked, "Are you fleeing Allāh's *qadar*?" indicates that acting upon the basis of cause and effect is a part of believing in Allāh's *qadar*. We know well that when a person says, "I believe in Allāh's destiny that I will have a child," but he does not get married, that such an individual would be classified as insane. Similarly, someone who says, "I believe in Allāh's destiny," but makes no effort to earn a living would be considered an idiot.

Belief in destiny does not negate the cause-and-effect laws pertaining to acts which have been commanded by the *Sharī'ah*, i.e., by Allāh's moral laws, nor the physical laws which govern the world in which we live in. We are talking about the material causes and effects that are real and authentic. However, those which are claimed but which are, in fact, imaginary, cannot be given consideration. They are not real, and no principles or concepts can be derived from them. I am talking about a problem that is in fact really not a problem, but people commonly raise it as an issue. They say, "If my deed is in accordance with Allāh's destiny, why should I then be punished for my sins."

سَيَقُولُ ٱلَّذِينَ أَشْرَكُوا۟
لَوْ شَآءَ ٱللَّهُ مَآ أَشْرَكْنَا وَلَآ ءَابَآؤُنَا وَلَا حَرَّمْنَا مِن شَىْءٍ ۚ
كَذَٰلِكَ كَذَّبَ ٱلَّذِينَ مِن قَبْلِهِمْ حَتَّىٰ ذَاقُوا۟ بَأْسَنَا ۗ
قُلْ هَلْ عِندَكُم مِّنْ عِلْمٍ فَتُخْرِجُوهُ لَنَآ ۖ إِن تَتَّبِعُونَ إِلَّا
ٱلظَّنَّ وَإِنْ أَنتُمْ إِلَّا تَخْرُصُونَ ﴿١٤٨﴾

"Those who worship others with Allāh will say, 'If Allāh willed otherwise we would not have worshipped others along with Him, nor our fathers, nor would we have had any taboos.' So did those before them argue falsely, until they tasted My wrath. Say: 'Have you any (certain) knowledge? If so, produce it before us. You follow nothing but conjecture: you do nothing but lie.' " Sūrah *al-An'ām* (6):148.

The response to that is that one cannot use destiny as a justification for disobedience to God. Allāh did not force the individual to commit his sins. When you set out to commit a sin, you did not have knowledge that it was destined for you, because a human being does not know what is destined for him until it takes place. Why didn't you think that Allāh had destined obedience and righteousness for you and do that instead - just as you strive in this material life to do what you consider to be good and best for you? Why doesn't the individual treat the affairs of the next life the same way that he treats the affairs of this life? If somebody told you that there were two ways to Makkah, one which was safe, smooth and easy, and the other one difficult and dangerous, no one would take the dangerous and difficult way and say, "This is what Allāh has destined for me." There is no difference between that and saying that there is a path to Paradise and there is a path to Hell. If you take the path to Hellfire, you are like the one who takes the path which is difficult and dangerous, so why do you then claim that it is Allāh's destiny that you take that path? Even if human beings had an argument with regards to destiny and their acts of disobedience, that argument is invalidated by the fact that Allāh has sent messengers and prophets so that there would not be any arguments, as Allāh said:

رُّسُلًا مُّبَشِّرِينَ وَمُنذِرِينَ لِئَلَّا يَكُونَ
لِلنَّاسِ عَلَى ٱللَّهِ حُجَّةُۢ بَعْدَ ٱلرُّسُلِۚ وَكَانَ ٱللَّهُ عَزِيزًا حَكِيمًا ﴿١٦٥﴾

> "Messengers who gave good news as well as warning, that humanity, after (the coming) of the messengers, should have no argument against Allāh. And Allāh is Ever-All Powerful, All-Wise." Sūrah *al-Nisā'* 4:165.

Belief in *qadr* has a beautiful result in the life of the individual. When things go well, the individual thanks Allāh and does not believe that whatever good things happened were just from his own effort. He will not be carried away by pride in his own strength, intelligence or skill to forget that he is ultimately the recipient of a favour from Allāh. Likewise, on the moral level, if a person does a good deed, he is not carried away by a sense of his own goodness. He realizes that he was only able to do so because Allāh guided him and gave him the ability to do the deed. This protects a person from feeling that he/she is doing Allāh a favour by doing good. Allāh said in the Qur'ān:

مَّآ أَصَابَكَ مِنْ حَسَنَةٍ فَمِنَ ٱللَّهِۖ

> "Whatever good comes to you is from Allāh." Sūrah *al-Nisā'* (4):79.

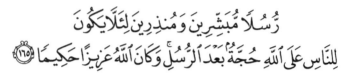

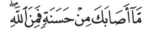

Similarly, when a person is tried by difficult times, belief in Allāh's destiny keeps him from falling into despair or wasting time and energy on an endless round of regrets and self-torture with thoughts of what may have been. The Prophet (ﷺ) told his nephew, "Know that if all humanity joined together to benefit you with something, they could not benefit you except with something that Allāh has already written for you; and that if all of humanity gathered to harm you, they could not harm you except by something that Allāh has already written for you. The pens have been lifted and the pages are dry."[248] In one version of the same *ḥadīth*, he said, "Know that what happened to you could not have been avoided and that what missed you could never have come to you." He also said, "Be eager for that which benefits you and don't be weak, but if something negative happens to you, don't say, 'If only...' for 'if only' opens the door for Satan."[249] A person who does not believe in *qadr* will, by contrast, be proud and deluded when good happens to him, and shattered by despair when trouble befalls him. The belief in *qadr* prevents all that.

The character that belief in Divine Decree builds is:

a) a patient personality

Knowledge that whatever happens is by God's decree gives one the ability to patiently bear the most difficult of times. When things do not go as planned, the believer accepts that God in His wisdom did not allow it to happen because it was not best.

There are so many cases in the West of people reacting violently to loss of jobs or wealth that psychiatrists are being brought in to jobs to teach workers how to deal with stress.

---

[248] Collected by *al-Tirmidhī*. See *Al-Nawawi's Forty Ḥadīth*, p. 68.

[249] *Ṣaḥīḥ Muslim*, 4:1401, no. 6441.

Investor goes on shooting spree, kills self

MIAMI, Florida, Tues (AP)

An investor who had suffered heavy stock market losses shot and killed a brokerage manager, wounded his personal broker, and then turned his gun on himself, police and witnesses said.

The gunman, Arthur Kane, 53, died at the scene of the shootings in the broker's offices yesterday, said police Cmdr. William Johnson. Kane was known as a regular customer.

The New York Post, quoting an unidentified Merrill Lynch source, said Kane "had as much as $8 million invested" in the stock market and that he "lost millions last week."

A Merrill Lynch spokesman said the slain brokerage manager was Jose Argilagos, 51. The wounded stock-broker was Lloyd Kolokoff, 39.

Both were vice-presidents of the local office.

Police said Kane was a social security hearing examiner for the federal government. Merrill Lynch employees said he visited their office nearly every day.

Melvyn Cohen, a Merrill Lynch vice-president, said Kane had received a "margin call' because of last week's decline. A margin call is to ask the client to put up more assets to cover the falling value of the stock. If the call is not met, the brokerage can sell the stock to cover the debt.

In Milwaukee, Wisconsin, a 58 year-old retired businessman, Vernon Lamberg, who reportedly lost $500,000 on the stock market in last week's crash has committed suicide.[250]

---

[250] *Saudi Gazette,* no. 3821, Oct. 28, 1987, p. 1.

Allāh addresses this in the Qur'ān saying:

وَلَنَبۡلُوَنَّكُم بِشَيۡءٖ مِّنَ ٱلۡخَوۡفِ وَٱلۡجُوعِ
وَنَقۡصٖ مِّنَ ٱلۡأَمۡوَٰلِ وَٱلۡأَنفُسِ وَٱلثَّمَرَٰتِۗ وَبَشِّرِ ٱلصَّٰبِرِينَ ١٥٥

> "And certainly, I will test you with some fear, hunger, loss of wealth, life and the fruit of your efforts so give glad tidings to those who are patient." Sūrah *al-Baqarah* (2):155.

b) a content personality

Knowledge that whatever wealth is gathered was already written gives the individual a sense of contentment when he or she fails in their efforts to gain more. The believer is encouraged to strive to attain the best of this world, but not at the expense of the next world. And after trying one's utmost, one then puts his or her trust in Allāh and accepts whatever comes.

Belief in the Destiny also keeps one from falling into despair or from being consumed with regrets and daydreams about what might have been.

The desire to have what others have cause many in the West to live far beyond their means through credit cards and buy-now-pay-later plans.

c) a stable personality

Awareness that whatever befalls the believer was already written and that it was all according to the permission of God causes the believer to have a stable personality. The believer remains free from the extremes of happiness that cause one to forget God and the extremes of sadness that causes the ignorant to lose hope and blame God. Consequently, both the trials of good and the tests of evil benefit the believer. Ṣuhayb ibn Sinān related that the Messenger of Allāh (ﷺ) said, "*The affair of the believer is amazing! The whole of his life is beneficial, and that is only in the case of the believer. When good times come to him, he is thankful and it is good for him, and when bad times befall him, he is patient and it is also good for him.*"[251] This is the state of one who has truly accepted God's destiny.

[251] *Ṣaḥīḥ Muslim,* vol. 4, p. 1541, no. 7138.

BIBLIOGRAPHY

Currie, P.M., *The Shrine and Cult of Mu'in al-din Chishti of Ajmer,* Delhi: Oxford University Press, 1992.

Farrington, Benjamin, *What Darwin Really Said,* London: Sphere Books, 1971.

Fenwick, Peter and Elizabeth, *The Truth in the Light,* New York: Berkeley, 1995.

Glynn, Patrick, *God The Evidence,* Rocklin, CA: Forum, Prima Publishing, 1997.

Huntington, Samuel P., *The Clash of Civilisations and the Remaking of World Order,* London: Touchstone Books, 1998

Sagan, Carl, *Broca's Brain,* New York: Random House, 1979.

The Runnymede Trust, *Islamophobia a challenge for us all,* England: The Runnymede Trust, 1997

The Living Webster Encyclopedic Dictionary of the English Language, Chicago: The English Language Institute of America, 1971

Colliers Encyclopedia, Macmillan Educational Company, NY, 1989.